Follows and Likes
Is This All That I'm Worth?

Understanding Success in the Age of Social Media

Kristi Maggio

First paperback edition October 2021
Maggio Multicultural Publishing

Book design by Kristi Maggio

ISBN 9781668583111 (paperback)
ISBN 2940162530589 (ebook)

www.maggiomulticulturalfoundation.org

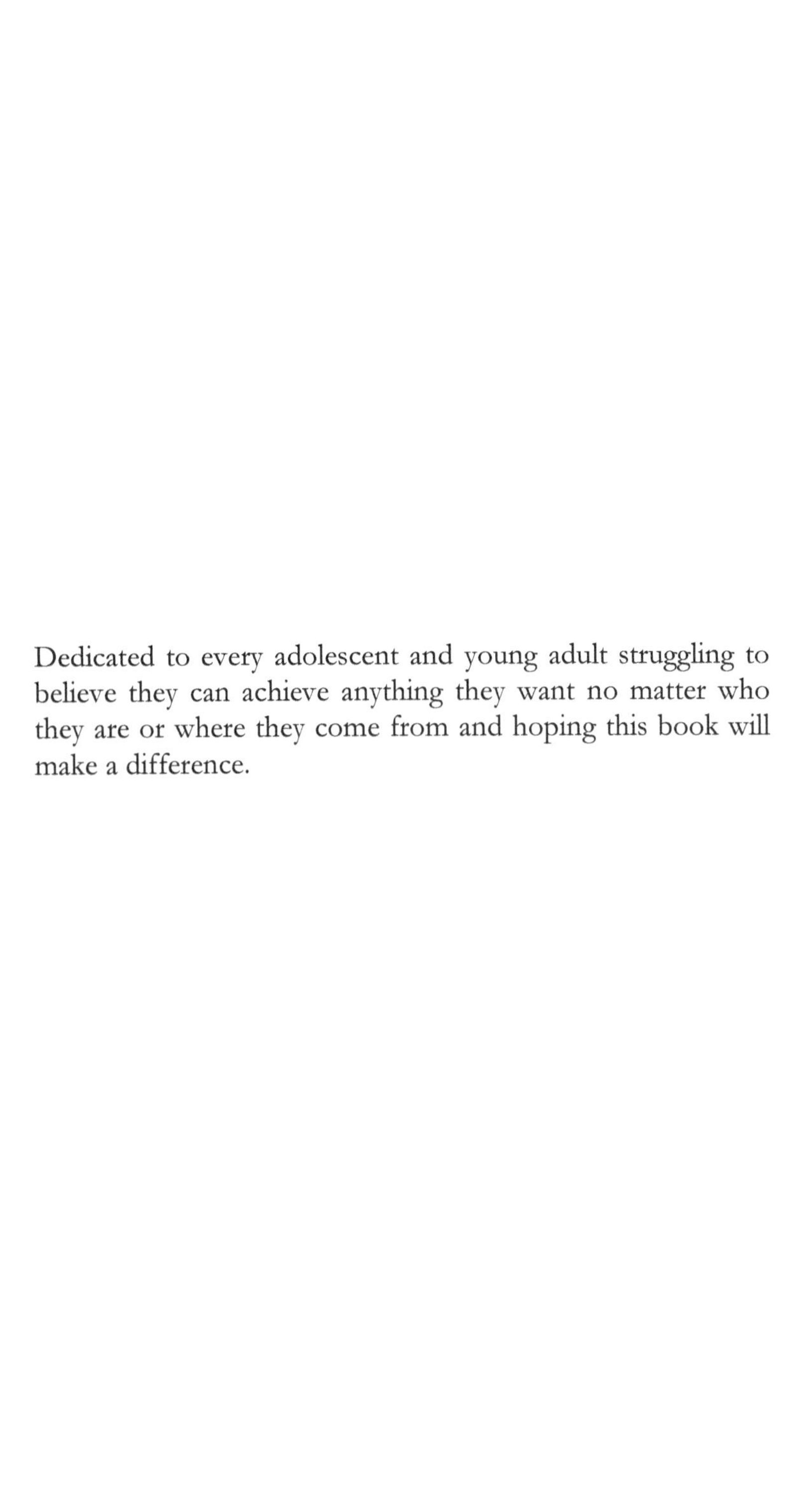

Dedicated to every adolescent and young adult struggling to believe they can achieve anything they want no matter who they are or where they come from and hoping this book will make a difference.

"Remember, the people that we praise in public have spent years and years in private working on their craft to achieve what they have. Don't get lost in the "feed." It's a filtered feed. We see the finished product. A person's success is like an iceberg. What you see at the surface, for example the images on social media, is just a small part of what is actually there. Meaning what you see today from someone you admire is the product of many other things that you have not seen in order for them to achieve what they have today."

— Ram Castillo

Table of Contents

Foreword

We are all imperfectly perfect. You might wonder, "What does that mean?" When you think of anyone in the world, any human at least, we would have to admit that everyone is imperfect. We all have flaws. Perfection does not exist, rather it is based on individual perspectives. It is merely in the "eye of the beholder." What one may see as perfect, another may see as not good enough.

Perfection can only be attained by God or the Divine, and when we think about it, this simply means that we are all the same, uniquely perfect in our own way. Just as a snowflake ceases to have an exact replica, every person is a special and unique individual.

Through my work as the founder of the Imperfectly Perfect Campaign, the mission has been to destigmatize mental health issues by showing that even those we revere as celebrities or important public figures have often battled with feeling less than perfect. So, it is with the work of people like myself, Kristi and all the amazing personalities in this book that I want to express to you that you are perfect just as you are.

You are exactly how you are meant to be, imperfectly perfect. So, don't allow that inner voice, or the voice of others, tell you anything different. Because if you can imagine a perfect world, hopefully the image of that world will love you for exactly who you are both inside and out.

Glenn Marsden

Every day young people fall prey to *"Compulsive Popularity Disorder."* There's a direct link between narcissistic, neurotic behavior and social media. Sadly, most of it stems from our desire to be "liked" and a "like button."

The negative effect this has on a young person's mental health is outstanding. It negatively impacts body image, increases bullying and "FOMO" (fear of missing out). It fuels anxiety, depression, and loneliness.

When Kristi told me about this book and her wish to include my story, I immediately jumped at the chance to spread this message. It's time we redefine success in the age of social media.

This book is a must read for Generation Z. When the world is constantly telling our youth to fit in Kristi declares, "Do not allow yourself to be labeled, prejudged, and stuffed into a box that is defined by someone else." I agree with her 1000 percent!

Ungenita Prevost

Introduction

"I've learned that people will forget what you said, people will forget what you did, but people will never forget how you made them feel."
- Maya Angelou

Do you think there is a correlation between social media and your self-worth? You may think so, or maybe not; or maybe you've never thought about it. In deciding to read this book, you may be hoping to learn how to be successful. You may be intrigued by the title of the book and love (or dislike) everything social media. Perhaps you think it will lead you to creating success like other people you see and admire, or simply because someone suggested it to you. Whatever the reason, allow yourself to go on a journey with the intention being that when you finish this book, you will know yourself better, you will feel more confident, and you will understand more clearly what you want and how to get it. Keep in mind that what you see on social media and how you allow it to affect you could be holding you back from your true potential.

Can you remember a time when you passed something up and wished you had the opportunity again? The good news is that opportunities come and go, so help in recognizing them is important. This book will help you make the choices that are right for YOU, not based on what your parents want, what society tells you that you should want, what you see on social media or what your peers are doing. The sole purpose is to ensure you are equipped with the right tools, mentally, physically, and emotionally as to not pass up opportunities that are presented to you or spend four years in university studying one thing, only to realize after the fact that you really wanted to do something else.

I am here to help you think critically about outside influences, and the value they have in your life to either lift you up and help you or break you down and hurt you. I am here so that the day doesn't come when you turn forty and have a moment of self-discovery and say, *"I wish I knew this years ago."* I am also here to make you truly believe that no matter who you are, where you come from, what your ethnicity is, if you come from a rich or poor family, have had a traumatic childhood experience, feel unloved, unwanted, are in foster care, an orphan, adopted, feel misunderstood, or are the most popular person in school, you will discover what true success is for you and how to achieve it just as much as anyone else can.

If you have been told anything different up until now about what you can accomplish in this life, if you have believed you are not meant for greatness, if someone said to you that the thing you love to do the most is stupid or can't be done, I'm telling you now that it's a lie, and I will prove it. You can achieve your dreams, and I have multiple examples, so you don't just have to take my word for it. Through the stories told at the end of each chapter, you will see for yourself.

Now I'm not an adolescent, but in writing this book, I write to my insecure adolescent self as well. I am that forty-year-old that asked herself, *"Why didn't I learn this sooner?"* I may be older than you, but I understand what you are going through. I have gone through a great many obstacles, yet I have overcome them, and I now think fondly of those obstacles. I actually appreciate the challenges I have faced. This might sound strange, but without them, I wouldn't be who I am today. I assure you I have felt every feeling you do.

I have been an educator for over 20 years, and my students love and respect me because of my authenticity and because they know I care. I hope through my words and the stories I share; you can feel it too. Every one of my students over the past twenty years, even the most difficult ones, have touched my life, and I theirs, in many ways. Many of my students have come to me in times of trouble and when they have needed help or advice. However, I can be honest and say that although I tried, I was not able to save them all. Some to this day are no further ahead; some are in jail, and a couple are dead.

So, my "why" in writing this book is to reach as many young people as I can and guide them to have the right skills and the right mindset on this journey called life. Do not allow yourself to be labeled, prejudged, and stuffed into a box that is defined by someone else. You have so much information coming at you from so many different sources. On one hand, it is a blessing to have it all at the touch of a button, and on the other hand, it is also difficult to distinguish what is real and what isn't. Make sure to always ask questions, analyze what you are being told, think critically, and look for help in understanding what you may not know.

In this book, you will be introduced to some amazing people and amazing stories of overcoming even the worst of situations. You will see why they chose the path to overcome their circumstances, not stay in victim mode, and how they created success and followed their dreams. So, let's get started!

<u>The Story of Greg Walker
Dream, Grind and Hustle</u>

"If there's anything in life that you want, all you gotta do is dream, grind and hustle because I truly believe each and every one of us are too big to dream small." – Greg Walker

Growing up, Greg Walker was teased and called the "Big Dreamer" because he always believed he would do great things even when those around him made fun of him and asked, "Who do you think you're gonna be? The one to make it out, really? No one ever passed so how are you gonna make it out?" He was called a mute and didn't actually speak until about the age of 12 because of things that his father and his siblings said to him. However, he had loving teachers who used to talk to him at school and used to tell him that he's not who his family is.

Greg is one of 15 children who grew up in inner city Columbus, Ohio. He comes from a family of drug abuse, alcoholism, sexual battery, anything you can name is part of that history. Growing up with a family of 15 where no one ever made it past 9th grade, his goal was to be the first one to ever graduate high school.

Picture this… On Greg's first day of high school, he sat there in class and the principal called to see him. He walked down to the office and just thought his parents didn't sign something, however that wasn't the case. The principal stood in front of him and said, "Greg, do you understand that you are number 13, and there were twelve of your siblings before you that didn't make it out? Do you understand that number 13 is an unlucky number, so if you think you're going to be the one who makes it out of this, you need to read books and study hard because the odds are against you?" The principal then threw down some papers and said, "those are the papers that your twelve siblings before you signed to drop out of the ninth grade, so they'll be ready for you."

It's shocking to think this was what the head of the school said to a student. Unfortunately, these instances do happen more frequently than anyone would like to admit. This person should have been encouraging Greg instead of bringing him down. Luckily for Greg he did have a few people who believed in him. If this is happening to you or has happened to you, stay strong and prove them wrong!

When Greg left the principal's office that day, he felt defeated. He was ready to fight and wanted to hit someone. He walked out the front door of the school with tears in his eyes. However, someone grabbed him from behind. It was his teacher who prayed for him. She looked at him and asked why he was crying. When he told her what happened, she went with him straight to the office, told Greg to wait outside, and she had words with that principal like he had never experienced before in his life. This is what the love of someone who cares can do to change your life.

This teacher always said, "Gregory you are not your family. You are not your father; you are not your brother or your mother or your sisters. You can be whoever you want to become." This teacher and others got him through high school. It wasn't easy, but he worked hard and was determined. There were moments he almost didn't make it. When you live in an environment like Greg lived in, it is difficult to think you are going to be anything other than what you are surrounded by. His own family told him he was stupid. He was bombarded by people who called him dumb and told him that he would be locked up like others in his family or become an alcoholic, drug addict or abuser of women.

Other than his teachers in high school, who would help him create a better life, he had another incredible mentor, Dave

Thomas. If you've never heard this name, I am sure you have heard of the fast-food restaurant Wendy's. Dave Thomas was the founder of Wendy's.

As a child, Dave was also told he would never succeed and called crazy for starting a hamburger chain when McDonald's and Burger King already existed. Dave gave Greg's 9th grade class the chance to work with him and be mentored by him or one of his staff members every Saturday to teach them about success. However, only three people showed up. Dave himself was a high school dropout who only made it to the tenth grade, but he had the opportunity to be mentored by the great Harland Sanders, founder of Kentucky Fried Chicken or KFC.

For Greg, the opportunity to be mentored by this incredible man, as well as the love and care of his teachers, were what he needed to be the first to graduate high school, but he didn't stop there. Greg tried college, but he didn't like it and wouldn't allow that to stop his success. Again, he was faced by naysayers telling him he could never be a businessperson, but once again he didn't listen and proved them wrong. Greg began to open restaurant franchises, including 270 taco franchises and ice cream stores.

Greg just kept going. He then joined Toastmasters, a worldwide organization that teaches competent communication and leadership skills. Les Brown, an incredible motivational speaker, became another mentor for Greg. After five months, he was competing, and he was now being told he had a gift for public speaking. Shocking to Greg, he was now getting paid to speak and motivate other people with his story. Today Greg has become a motivational speaker and bestselling author with the help and encouragement of Toastmasters and the amazing Les Brown.

His advice, "Just remember you are not defined by those around you or those who have come before you. I went from graduating last in my class to receiving an honorary doctorate's degree! Wishes do come true if you are willing to dream, grind and hustle." Believe in yourself and surround yourself with good people. You can't change who your family is or who you have to live with, but you can ignore them. If you don't believe you can, just remember Greg's story; find a mentor to help you and surround yourself with people who will support you and who want to do great things too.

1

<u>Follows and Likes…
Do They Really Matter?</u>

"Success is personal, so stop comparing your apples to their oranges."
– Yohancé Salimu

Social media is everywhere. It can't be avoided, and it is here to stay. Like anything in this world, all things are good in moderation, and too much of anything can have consequences. Social media has helped connect the world and people you otherwise may have not contacted or seen again for years. It allows families who live apart to come together. It is a great resource for raising awareness for different causes and social impact campaigns. Yet it is also a stomping ground for hate, negativity, bullying and blatant lies.

So let me ask you… What do you look for when you scroll through social media? Are you checking to see what other people are doing? Are you looking to compare your life with others? When you post something, what is it that you usually post? If you post a selfie, what do you hope will happen? How do you feel when posting or when scrolling? Stop and answer these questions and if you aren't sure, then take note the next time you scroll or post. Do the number of follows or likes you get have a big impact on your mood, and if so, why?

Picture this… Let's say you take a selfie, you put it through filters, add emojis or take it multiple times to be just right. Before sending it, you know it can go either two ways, it will be uplifting or deflating. This goes through your head over and over again, but you finally just click "post." Now, the waiting begins. Ask yourself, do you feel anxiety after you post something or just post for fun? What are your expectations for posting?

9

How often do you look at social media with feelings of jealousy or envy possibly wishing you could be someone that you follow on there or wishing that your life was as "perfect" as theirs? Hopefully not often, but if you do compare regularly, let me let you in on a little secret. The life that you think seems so perfect, isn't as perfect as you think. What you see is an illusion. It is what you have created them to be in your imagination. It is the life you dream for yourself that you are projecting onto others, thinking that they have it and not you.

Why? Because we have been programmed to believe something that doesn't really exist. How many people do you know that would post a picture of themself having a bad day? How many people do you know that would post themself just after getting in an argument with someone else or crying or seeming like their life is terrible and unworthy of living? Not many that I know of. What we see on social media is the illusion of happiness and success, yet very little of it is what you believe it is.

Now I am not saying that people aren't happy when they post or that everything is fake, because it's not. What I am saying is that no one can be perfectly happy, perfectly beautiful, perfectly good looking, or perfectly successful all the time. As you keep wanting or imagining the life that others have, I am suggesting from this moment on you stop and start looking for what is missing inside of you, instead of externally.

Now let's go back to that post you just sent and look at the two main outcomes that could possibly happen.

Outcome Number 1: An hour has gone by and without much activity. You get a couple of likes from your closest "peeps" but not what you were hoping for, so you start to make up scenarios in your head as to why there haven't been more reactions when you know your "friends" have been online. The reasons come pouring in… they haven't seen it; there is something wrong with the picture; nobody really likes you… and the list goes on and on. You have literally drained yourself and feel worthless.

Outcome Number 2: The likes and comments of how great the post is and how wonderful you look come pouring in, and you feel rejuvenated and alive, and feel as though you could conquer the world and have a life worth living just like all of the other "happy" people on social media. You feel priceless… for now.

May I ask… what on earth are you doing to yourself? What has caused this inner questioning about who you are and what you are worth? Why do you feel that the number of follows and likes that you receive somehow equate to your self-worth? Well, it is mostly because that is what you are bombarded with every second of every day.

Just writing that section turned my insides out! I know what it feels like, wanting to be more, do more, look better and have that internal gratification from external sources. The rush you get when someone friends or likes your post, the thrill of the great comment you weren't expecting puts you on cloud nine!

I also know the flipside. Obsessing after a break-up to see if your former significant other has posted anything or been active. Feeling down one day and taking a selfie, just to put it through a filter so you look flawless and more attractive to boost your self-esteem. Posting pictures so the girls or guys that excluded you from a certain activity will be jealous because you are doing something without them.

This behavior will exhaust you and none of it is going to make you feel better about yourself in the long term. However, I will tell you what it will do. It will consume you to the point where you feel like you are going crazy and cannot concentrate on anything other than what you think other people think about you, and let's be honest… who cares! The more important question is, what do you think about yourself?

You need not care what other people think about you, actually what other people think about you is none of your business, and you will always have someone that doesn't like you no matter how hard you try. You need to care about what you think about you and live your life with meaning and purpose. Ask yourself… was I a good person today? Was my day productive? Did I live today with integrity and honesty? Was I kind or did I help someone? Did I accomplish my goals for today? Was I kind to myself today, meaning did I have positive self-talk, eat healthy, do some sort of exercise, even if for a short time? If you do most or all of these things on a daily basis, then you are more successful than most people.

If you think that you are not successful, beautiful, worthy, or popular then your idea of real success is based on a distorted image of reality, and it's time to look deep inside and start working on who you are and discover why you feel this way. So, let's reflect to dig a little deeper! Describe the person that you think you are. Describe the person that you think others think you are. Write it down.

Are your answers the same or different? Why or why not? Be honest! This is between you and you. So, lying to yourself doesn't help.

How do you feel about what you see on social media? Do you compare your life with what you see, or find yourself wishing you could be someone or something different? If so, why? What do you wish you had in your life, or who do you wish you could be? What do you think they have that you don't? What characteristics do they have that you are looking to have yourself?

Luckily for me, I had a friend who helped me understand that follows and likes don't equal success. Remember we often see the glamorous life that people live now, but look at any celebrity or wealthy person today, and I will tell you that the road to their success was not straight and narrow, nor was it easy and paved with gold. So, never think that what someone has today or what you see on social media is something they always had and didn't work for. Everyone started at the bottom, many with traumatic experiences. Then they worked their way to what they have today. They broke through the trauma. Nothing began as glitz and glam. So, if you are looking for the easy road to success, there are very few. However, the good news is no matter who you are or where you come from, you can achieve anything you want in this life.

Therefore, what do you want and what action are you taking to get there?

<u>The Story of Ungenita Prevost
From Product of the Projects… to a
Billion Dollar Rolodex</u>

"We have a choice; we can continue to ignore foster children or deal with the ramifications of our actions when they 'age out' of the foster care system. Minorities, gays, trans-genders, refugees, immigrants, and women are all groups of people our society rallies behind, yet foster children continue to go unnoticed. No one wants to deal with "parentless children," or better yet, a child that has been labeled flawed by society. It's time to stop treating foster children like they are invisible. They deserve to perfect their potential. If you'd like to see a decrease in homelessness, human trafficking, incarceration, and unemployment in our society, transforming foster care is a powerful solution." – Ungenita Prevost

From product of the projects. to foster care, to Hollywood and now a successful entrepreneur, Ungenita Prevost's story starts when her biological father took her from her biological mother and left her on the doorstep of his girlfriend who became her surrogate mother. From the age of two until her early teen years, her life was fairly normal, even though she lived in the projects and ate off food stamps. Many days were filled with grilled cheese sandwiches, from what she would call "government cheese" that came in a big block. She gives a lot of credit to her surrogate mom, because she tried her best to make Ungenita feel wanted.

When Ungenita began school, she always felt different, but she didn't know or realize why at the time. Even today she tells adults who are foster parents or educators of foster children to be very careful, because they can sense when they don't feel as though they belong. Until she was twelve her life was stable, but the day came when this all changed forever.

One day, Ungenita's surrogate mom had a seizure and died suddenly. This left Ungenita alone. Through a series of events after her surrogate mother's death and because her biological father was in and out of her life, she was to be reunited with the biological mother whom she had never met. This was the start of a completely different life for Ungenita, and she was uprooted and moved to California.

Ungenita always had dreams inside of her. She knew that she was going to do great things. In California, she attended Catholic school and that was comfort because she had already been in Catholic school and was able to make some great friends. However, the good times didn't last long, and Ungenita and her mother were not getting along. Her mother didn't act like a mother and just wasn't fit or ready to have a child. It was hard for Ungenita to adjust, going from being raised by a woman who loved her unconditionally but wasn't her real mother, to living with the woman who was her biological mother and couldn't care less about her.

One day the police showed up at school and took Ungenita to a shelter because her mother had been reported for child abuse. At this time, Ungenita was 15 years old. Although her mom was not physically abusive, it was emotional abuse and neglect that ultimately led to Ungenita entering the children's shelter and the foster care system. Once again, her life was uprooted. In an interview, she stated, "I can remember this vividly like it was yesterday. I remember walking in, and you know they register you or whatever they do right in the office, and then you go into a room that looks like camp, but it's a room filled with beds and a locker. That's where you sleep with the other girls. During the day, you go to school at the shelter."

Ungenita was in the shelter for several months, going through child welfare services and the court system. She was assigned a social worker, and after a couple of months, she had to go to court with her biological mother. They were trying to decide if she would be returned to her mom or if she would stay in the custody of the state, however Ungenita didn't want to go back. She felt she was becoming a young lady and didn't feel right about returning, but the system wanted her to go back. She then had to go to court again, and as they were going to place her back with her mother, something happened to her mother, and she wasn't granted custody again. Therefore, Ungenita went back into the system, and that is where she stayed until she aged out at 18.

Ungenita lived with incredible young girls who were also "unwanted" children. Many were molested by their fathers or abused by their mothers. Some of them were from homes with parents who were addicts or alcoholics or were physically abused. Some had parents who died, and the next of kin were unable to care for them. As Ungenita recalls, "these girls were good girls with their share of problems, but just in need of love and caring. Some of the girls were serial runaways, used to living on the streets and hitchhiking to get away. In reality, many of them disappeared most likely getting kidnapped and used in human trafficking. If they managed to survive until their eighteenth birthday, they were given the gift of aging out of the system and left to manage on their own with zero support. Most of these girls end up in jail, on drugs, or mothers on welfare." Ungenita was one of the few to make it out and not become a statistic.

At a young age, Ungenita started working. She knew her day to age out would come, and she would only have herself to depend on, so she made sure she was ready. She had a desire to do something with her life. She was a dreamer, and she was also intelligent. She realized to make it she needed the right skills, so she put herself in situations where she could develop life skills like communication, sales, and networking. On the day she had to leave the system, she needed to survive. She needed a place to live; she needed to buy food and buy a bus pass, as she didn't have a car. She only had some clothes and a few toiletries. Luckily, a friend found a room for her to rent.

Ungenita had it in her that she wanted to go to Hollywood like so many young people, and she moved to San Francisco to start modeling. She got some fashion show jobs and an agent, and with less than a thousand dollars, she found a ride and a sofa to sleep on, and she made it to Hollywood. She went to auditions and was fortunate enough to get her first job just days after she started attending casting calls. She attributes this to her ability to network.

Ungenita went on to do incredible work. She appeared in several music videos including LL Cool J, Black Eye Peas, and the late Robert Palmer. She was a double for Janet Jackson, had roles in movies like *Homegrown* with Bon Jovi and Billy Bob Thornton, *Dude Where's My Car* with Ashton Kutcher, and she even worked with Steven Spielberg in the movie *Amistad*. Ungenita never gave up; she never believed she would only be a statistic. Deep within she knew she was meant for greatness, and she has created her success despite the odds that were against her. She has been homeless, jobless, carless, cashless, and made it without a mother or a father.

Today, Ungenita teaches female entrepreneurs how to build social capital and monetize their networks. She hosts the online summit "Ms. Popular Vs. Ms. Profitable." She teaches people to stop chasing fans, followers, likes and subscribers and giving your financial power away to a "like" button. Why? Because being popular on social media might be great for the ego, but if it's not great for your bank account as well, then it doesn't really matter. It's about the quality of your network, not the quantity of your network, and this is how she created her success. She says, "Social capital—not your financial capital—is the most valuable asset you can have."

2

<u>Compare and Contrast…</u>
<u>Proceed at Your Own Risk!</u>

"To be yourself in a world that is constantly trying to make you something else is the greatest accomplishment." – Ralph Waldo Emerson

Now that we have uncovered a little bit of your perception about yourself and the world of social media, let's dig deeper in the world of comparison. Let's think again about how often you compare what you have with what someone else has. How often do you wish your life was more like someone else's or wish you had what they have? How often do you put others down or talk about them behind their back out of personal insecurity, jealousy or because you honestly feel you are better than they are? Comparing ourselves to others is not a good idea. Why? Because there is no one like you and there is no one like me. No one has walked in your shoes, and you have not walked in someone else's shoes to truly understand another person's perspective.

We are all completely unique individuals, and by comparing our similarities and differences to others, we are most likely doing it to make ourselves feel better at the other person's expense, or we are doing it and the result is that we feel worse about ourselves because in our mind he or she is somehow better than we are. We often take for granted what we have and want what other people have, and I will give you the perfect example of understanding the difference of perspective.

Growing up as a white woman, being tanned was a beautiful thing. Many white people pay a lot of money during the winter months to have that golden brown skin tone or spend vacations on sunny islands lying in the sun most of the time. Many white people think that those who are golden brown are so lucky because they are the perfect shade of brown. Right? Wrong! It wasn't until I moved to the Dominican Republic and was around other Dominican people that I got a whole new perspective. In the beginning, I never understood the reason they don't like being out in the sun and often cover themselves as much as possible to not be in the sun. Why…you might ask? Because being a lighter shade of brown is a social status. In their culture, the lighter you are comes with the idea that you are wealthier. It might sound crazy, but to them being lighter means you aren't low-skilled labor, working outside in the sun all day. I was shocked and thought it was crazy to think that way, but it's true. Interesting, isn't it?

Another perfect example is size and figure. In many countries, people aim to be thin and think the perfect body is one that has little curve to it. However, in other countries, the Dominican Republic included, beauty has curves. In some countries, people pay to have liposuction to take the fat out, and in other countries, people pay to put the fat in and have injections to make specific areas of their body more voluptuous. You must realize that while you may be wishing to have what someone else has, someone else is out there wishing to have what you have.

Social media, and what some think is beautiful or trendy, can make you crazy. People see what others have, what an influencer or A-list celebrity has, and automatically want it too. We put others down and say things we shouldn't. We criticize, judge and gossip about others either because we want what they have or to make ourselves feel better. Think about the last thing you saw on your social media feed. What were your thoughts? If you don't remember, then be conscious of it next time you look. What are you saying about what you are seeing? Write down the first thing that comes to your mind with each post you see. Then count how many are negative comments and how many are positive. Hopefully you have more positive thoughts than negative ones.

Comparing yourself and others to an idea that you have in your mind about what should and should not be is a dangerous thing. You are setting yourself and others up to a standard that will ultimately fail. Wanting others to hurt should not make you feel better about yourself! As well, you should not think you are any less than anyone else, as you are a unique individual, and there is no one in this world exactly like you. Nothing should make you feel better if it is at the expense of someone else's feelings. Everyone has fear, anxiety, doubt and feelings of low self-esteem at some point or another no matter how popular he or she is. If you think the people you admire don't have the same worries, anxiety, and frustrations that you do, think again.

Are you noticing a pattern? A great majority of adolescents and adults are comparing their lives to others, wanting what others have and looking for ways to make themselves feel better whether it is real or not. How then is it possible for anyone to truly know what will make them happy, or feel good about themselves for an extended period of time, if they are constantly looking on the outside for instant, inner gratification? Why do people think a certain person or way of life is what is right, glamorous, or successful? Where did this belief come from?

At the end of the day, we should all live by one simple rule, and you probably learned it in your first years of school. It is the simple Golden Rule! Do unto others as you would want to have done unto you. Imagine if we all lived by this one simple rule how different the world would be!

I want to go one step further and bring to your mind an adapted form called the golden rule from Jones of Toledo which is, "what I want for myself I want for everybody else."

Think about that. Imagine if I want to be prosperous and grow, and I want to have great things happen to me, then I want that for everybody. That wipes out unhealthy competition, comparison, jealousy, and desire for what other people have. So, when you can think like that and lift people up, you ultimately lift yourself up at the same time because it's kindness in your heart.

We should all be here living together in a way that will serve each other not in a way to tear somebody else down so that we can get one step ahead. You can think of that when you are part of a team, in a class, applying to university, or in any industry; truly wanting the best for someone and for yourself is really what it's all about. So, the next time you are comparing yourself to someone else, putting yourself down because you want to be that person, or the next time you are being critical because you're jealous, you really need to look within and find what's going to shift that way of thinking and fill that void you have inside.

I think a good place to start today is to think of that person that maybe you always wish you have what they have, and say to yourself, I'm happy for them, and I'm going to have that too someday. Today is the day to appreciate you for you and love the person you are.

The Story of Dr. Jen Welter Who Said There Can't Be Females in Football?

"Whenever someone says it's impossible, it's impossible only because someone hasn't done it yet. You could be that one person that does it if it's truly within your heart and soul to do it." – Dr. Jen Welter

Throughout history, females have always been compared to their male counter parts as inferior. While the twentieth century brought great strides to changing the way women are viewed, there is still a long way to go before complete equity is seen between the two, and one place that is predominantly a male world is in sports. However, there have been those iconic women who are paving the way for the younger generations of girls to be seen as an equal instead of an inferior counterpart, and one of these women is Dr. Jen Welter.

Dr. Jen Welter is the first female NFL coach in history, proving that when anyone says, "you can't," or "it has never been done before," her story is one to bring inspiration and hope to say there is always a first for everything! It was in football where Jen heard for the first time that there was a difference between what girls could do and what boys could do, and she has made it her mission to break the stereotypes for other girls growing up. However, the journey to get to this moment of equity and strength was a difficult one, powered by extreme desire, determination, and the love of the game.

As a child growing up, Jen always wanted to be either an actress or an athlete. She loved competition; she was excellent in math and anything that she had to do to compete just drove something inside of her. She always related to the spicy characters in books and plays, and she loved to be social and do as much as possible that she could on her own.

The inspiration of Jen Welter comes from her drive and perseverance. However, before football, there was tennis. She loved tennis, but her coach told her that she would never do anything good or amount to anything because she was too short. You see Jen is only five feet two inches tall. That is correct! She is very small not just for tennis but for football as well, which makes her story that much more amazing.

Her thoughts on what young people should do when they are told by adults that they can't or that they will never make it, she says, "Whenever someone says it's impossible, it's impossible only because someone hasn't done it yet. You could be that one person that does it if it's truly within your heart and soul to do it."

For her whole life, Jen was told she was too small to play rugby and football, but she ended up playing both. She knew she couldn't control her height, but there were things that she could control. She couldn't make herself any taller, however she could make herself stronger and by making herself stronger, she was able to play in a different way by using her strength. She would go to the gym and make sure that she was able to be stronger. She would work on her speed, and she could get faster. This she could control to make herself more competitive and give herself a better edge.

It was hard to be part of a world that did not recognize what she did or what she was doing. There were times when Jen would live out of her car because she wasn't paid to play on the woman's professional league. It's interesting to think that she was on a professional sports team, and she and her teammates would have to raise money to support the team, but she still kept going. Jen was often knocked down, but she never failed, and she never failed because she refused to quit.

Her advice, "You need to take those little steps into understanding what it is that you want. Don't just automatically start with the big picture in mind because it's going to be more difficult. Take your goal and break it down into things you can achieve in windows, in small successes, in order to get you to the big goal."

Reflection is important to Jen in accomplishing her goals. Reflecting allows her to look at the good and not so good that has happened throughout the day and understand why. Doing this every day, brings great insight. For example, once prior to a game, she knew her team was going to beat the other team. Jen's team was the better team, however to their surprise, they lost. In looking back on the game and watching the replay, she realized the other team was better prepared. The other team knew them better, studied them better, knew the plays better, and even though they weren't as strong, they ultimately won because they knew their strategies and moves better than Jen's team knew theirs.

The moral to this story that she wants people to understand is that sometimes when you think somebody might be smarter than you, or somebody might be better than you or stronger than you, that doesn't necessarily mean that there isn't a way for you to win over that person, team or whatever it is you want in your life.

Today, Jen continues to coach and loves doing youth camps. She writes children's books that she claims some have done well and others not the greatest, but if her niece likes them, then that's all that counts. She continues to bridge the gaps and break the stereotypes for girls and will continue to fight for gender equality in sports.

3

Beware the Green-Eyed Monsters…
Jealousy and Envy

"Envy blinds men and makes it impossible for them to think clearly."
– Malcolm X

A lot of our actions come from what has been known over the years as the "green-eyed monster," jealousy or envy. Shakespeare first used the phrase in Othello. It was thought that such sentiment brought about illness and a green tint to the skin. Chaucer and Ovid use the term as well "green with envy." Jealousy and envy make people do crazy things. It doesn't matter if you are just an everyday person, the most popular boy or girl at school, the neighbor with everything, a celebrity, or anyone else you can think of, these two characteristics can make people go COO-COO… so watch out!

You might be asking what's the difference between the two? According to Google, jealousy is defined as feeling or showing desire to be someone or have their achievements and advantages. Envy is a feeling of discontented or resentful longing aroused by someone else's possessions, qualities, or luck. They are obviously synonyms, however, envy has more of a negative undertone as the person with envy doesn't feel good about themself and actually resents the other person who has what they want.

Jealousy and envy can easily make us frustrated, angry, or even depressed. However, ask yourself what it is that you are jealous about. Can you not have what other people have? Can you not do what others do? Perhaps not in the exact moment that you want it, but eventually you can. You can have exactly what anyone else has. Well, perhaps not exactly, but the idea is there. It's just not going to look exactly the same, and why would you want it to?

You can have great grades, a good-looking boyfriend, a beautiful girlfriend, a super job, lots of friends, be more athletic, have lots of things, if that's what you want. However, everything in the previous list is superficial. What would a beautiful boyfriend or girlfriend be if they weren't kind or loving to you? What would a high paying job be if you hated being at it every day? What would be great about having lots of friends if you aren't sure if they like you for you or if they like you for your money or popularity? What is the point of being the best athlete if you are only doing it for your parents or for popularity?

So, we must go back to WHY we are envious of someone or something and see if that why will give us enough motivation and desire to put forward the effort to achieve the end result, whatever it may be. Everything depends on desire, perseverance, and patience.

If you want your life to change overnight, then I hate to be the bearer of bad news, however, it's not going to happen (unless maybe you have a fairy godmother). However, you can start taking steps to stop being jealous of what other people have and begin creating it for yourself.

Start by looking around you. You can easily start with two things that you have with you every day, a good attitude and motivation. It is important to stop looking merely at the surface of what people have. Looks aren't always what they seem to be. Many people play the role of looking as though they have it all, however it is just a façade. They could be in huge debt and be a slave to their bills every month just because they want to look as though they have what all their friends have. This is called - *Keeping up with the Jones'*, - and with this mentality, you will never be satisfied. Someone will always have something different or better than you do, and you will always want more.

Love you for who you are. Don't be surface deep. Look into the people you envy and find out how they got to where they are today. Always stay true to yourself and never be tempted by fame, fortune, or greed. They will take you down a road that you don't want to go down. There is no quantity of popularity, money, follows or likes that is worth losing your honesty or integrity for. However, exploring and understanding your potential is key, as well as having the right mindset or attitude. Tell yourself everyday all the things you can do and will do, instead of all the things you can't do or all of the things that you aren't, which as you can imagine, will only hinder your progress forward in a healthy way.

In order to get what it is that you want, you must think of what motivates you. Motivation is important because if you aren't motivated to get what you want, then you are most likely setting the wrong goals for yourself, so let's ask the question, "how bad do I want it?" Whatever "IT" is. If you don't want something bad enough, it is likely that nothing will change. You must discover what truly makes you excited about getting up every day, or else you will lack the motivation and desire to achieve your goals.

Just remember there are certain steps you need to take in order to get what you want and not have a heart filled with jealousy or envy anymore, but none of these steps include hurting other people or yourself. If you want something, then do it with honesty and integrity or don't do it at all. Once you realize that you have the same capabilities as everyone else, then you will start seeing the world around you in a whole different light.

The Story of Barbara Majeski
Finding Strength in Adversity

"You grow through what you go through because it's going to help you serve and be a better person in the long run." - Barbara Majeski

Growing up, Barbara Majeski didn't have the same things that her friends had. She was often the "charity case" and had to wear "hand me downs" while her friends always had the newest things and the nicest clothes. Without a doubt she understands what many teenagers and young people go through. Being on the other side of charity as a teen and receiving presents that were donated to her family, she realized that she never wanted to be on this side of charity again. She wanted to be the one who had enough to give to others. Everything she did receive she appreciated, but at a young age, she realized that this wasn't the place where she wanted to stay. Her anger and envy fueled her drive to be the incredible success she is today.

As a child, Barb was put into the role of caretaker for her brother, Steven, who had a neurological disorder called Fragile X. She has dedicated her life to her younger brother, and at 6 years old when her mother told her Steven would never be able to speak, she vowed to always speak for him and ensure he would never want for anything. Growing up with a brother who had special needs shaped her and motivated her to make sure he would always have the best care.

Experiencing adversity at such a young age can be traumatizing, because as a child you don't understand why certain things happen, and there is a tendency to live in fear, anxiety, doubt, and frustration. From her experiences, she wants young people to know that every challenge that you encounter is there to help you grow. It is not there to break you; it is there to build you. If you look at these challenging experiences as ways to serve others, you will understand that you went through it for a reason. She says, "you grow through what you go through because it's going to help you serve and be a better person in the long run."

Everything Barbara has ever gone through has given rise to a greater purpose, and now in retrospect, she is grateful for all the adversities. They have been the fuel that have helped her achieve higher levels of success than her peers by allowing her to rise above mediocrity, financially, spiritually, and emotionally. However, it is important to take that perspective because adversity, tragedy and trauma can also keep you stuck as a victim of your circumstances. It is up to you as to whether those experiences will ultimately break you or build you.

At the age of 10, her parents divorced, and Barbara and her siblings were divided between New Jersey and California. She was in California for over a year with her father, and her brother Steven was always with her. At the age of 14, she wanted to return to start her freshman year of high school with her friends, and she fought to stay with her brother no matter what happened. It was a lot for a teenage girl to handle; from a tantrum in an airport, to setting the kitchen on fire, to dealing with her parents' divorce and having no money, she grew up quickly to take on a very maternal role. She swore time and again that she would never let her brother down, that she would make it big in the world and do whatever it takes. In high school, she lived in a studio apartment with her mom, 3 siblings, and their dog.

The vow of coming through for her brother whether conscious or subconscious helped her through everything. Every time she wanted to quit, she always remembered she couldn't because of her promise to Steven. Her rage and anger towards her parents were ever present in her teenage years. She grew up with very little, wearing hand-me-downs, moving from one side of the country to the other, and her needing to be more of the parent than her parents. She went without a great many things, but the difficult part was being surrounded with friends who had everything.

Her advice to young people, "In order to remove yourself from the adversity and the tragedy that life brings to you, you must hone the mindset that you are in control. However, it is not easy because we are conditioned by who we are surrounded by most, and we usually take on the beliefs of our parents and other family members and adopt how they think."

Barbara had to work very hard to reprogram her mind to accomplish her dreams and come through for her brother and for herself. She put herself through college and then went into the workforce, but she knew she couldn't take just any job if she was going to stay true to her promise that she made to herself and most importantly to her brother. Deep within, she knew she had to find an opportunity, and she did that in sales.

Barbara found people that were doing better than her to teach her what she needed to know. She worked hard, outworked everyone she knew, and followed people who were driven, aspirational and those who are big walkers and big talkers. She aligned herself with winners, and she knew she had to grow and take smart risks. She makes it very clear that there are no "get rich quick" schemes. You must find great people and tune out negative people that aren't aligned with what you are striving for.

Barbara did make it and was able to get into a very successful company from the ground. People told her she was crazy, it was a scam, it wouldn't amount to anything, but it turned out to be the great something she was looking for. She married and became a proud mother of 3, but as we often learn, once you achieve success, life has its ups and downs, twists and turns, and this was the same for Barbara.

At the age of 42, Barbara was diagnosed with Stage 3 Colon Cancer, and she went through hell. As well at the same time, she was going through a divorce. She didn't know what was going to happen, but she knew she wasn't going to give up without a good fight because her kids needed her and even more so, her brother Steven needed her. She often says that it wasn't Steven who needed her, but that she needed Steven. He brought out her strength and determination so that he could have the best in this world.

Barbara beat the cancer. She overcame her adversities, and today you will often see her on the *Today Show* and other shows as the lifestyle expert. She says her superpower is resilience. "Recognize that your purpose often shows up in the most traumatic events and hardships. Everyone is gifted with a purpose; you just have to find it and allow it to evolve."

4

The Choices We Make

"May your choices reflect your hopes, not your fears." - Nelson Mandela

The choices we make in our lives all have different outcomes. The choice plus the action taken equals some result. Sometimes it is good and other times, not so good. However, everything is about perspective. When was the last time you did something and loved the outcome? Now, think about the last time you did something and weren't as pleased with the results? The easiest thing to think of might be a time when you studied for something, put effort into it and got a good grade. The other might be a time you chose not to study, didn't put forth any effort and got a bad grade. Both began with a choice, whether or not to study. Both were followed by an action, studying or doing something else, and finally, both had an outcome, you either did or didn't do well.

The choices and decisions you make will shape your life. Sometimes you will choose to do something thinking the result will be one way, and it actually turns out in a completely different way. This will happen. However, whether the outcome is what you expected it to be or not, you need to then reflect on what you did and its outcome to understand what went well or what went wrong. Sometimes there are things that are out of your control and sometimes you may not take into account other factors which give you a different end result. An important thing to do before making any decision is start with the end in mind. What result do you want and why?

When you picture the result before choosing to do something, it can help you ultimately make the right decision. Let's go with a major decision that most of us have made or will make in our lifetime, whether or not to go to college or university. Unfortunately, young people are bombarded by the questions, *'what do you want to be'* or *'where do you want to go to school after you graduate,'* from the time they are toddlers. So how do you make such a crucial decision for your life when you are being pressured by those around you, and you have limited and bias information? You need to turn them off!

What do I mean by that? Consult yourself first. Think about what you truly want in your life or what truly interests you and make a list. It doesn't matter what it is; it could be eating ice cream (taste testers do exist). Then with all of those things on your list, what do you love the most. Finding your why and purpose of doing something is what will keep you going because if not, you will most likely lose interest in what you are doing. Therefore, doing what someone else wants you to do is not a good idea, something that parents often seem to forget.

After you have made your list, you may need to do a little investigation, and outweigh the pros and cons. For example, you might like to take care of kittens, so perhaps you would investigate being a veterinarian. Maybe you like to swim; so, you could look into marine biology or underwater photography. The possibilities are endless; however, I challenge you to go one step further in not just thinking about yourself, but also thinking about others and asking, *"what problem do I want to solve that will not only help me but will also help millions of people?"* This can bring a huge shift in thinking; you can be solving a real-world problem and love what you are doing at the same time.

In the end, when making life changing decisions about your future, make sure you take in all the information that you can and what you need to do to get there. Expose yourself to as many things as possible. When you hear about something new or are offered to try something for the first time, take the opportunity to learn more about it or do it. You never know!

It might be the opportunity you have been waiting for or the thing that ignites the fire within. As well, seek advice from those who are already doing what you may be interested in doing. Don't seek advice from people that do not have goals or aren't motivated to do great things, because they are not going to be the right people to listen to.

Whatever choice you are making, big or small, just remember to have the end in mind. This goes with social media as well. When scrolling, ask yourself, why? When posting something, ask yourself, why? 'Just because' isn't an answer. Just like Newton's Law, "Every action has an equal and opposite reaction." The more you put in, the more you will get out. The less you put in, the less you will get out. Even the smallest change will eventually have a ripple effect as time goes on. One moment, one choice, one decision can drastically alter the course of your life. So, make your choices wisely! The important thing to take away at this moment is that at any moment, your mindset can change in any direction depending on how motivated you are in making it happen.

The Story of Herb "Flight Time" Lang
Choose the Life You Want to Lead

"I will never ask a person to do something I am not willing to do myself. If I'm telling you, I'm showing you." – Herb Lang

Just like everyone in life we are faced with making difficult choices, and at a young age, Herb Lang was faced with difficult decisions that could have had very different outcomes. As a young boy from the projects in the small town of Brinkley, Arkansas, Herb never imagined that one day he would travel the world as a Harlem Globetrotter, meet the Pope and presidents of the United States, be on the TV show the *Amazing Race*, or become an author. However, he did just that and more! His life as a child was filled with challenges, as many are. He was born to a teenage mom who had six children by the time she was 25, and although she couldn't give her children everything they wanted, she did give them everything they needed.

Herb's mother instilled in him a lot of perseverance along the way, and it forced him to never give up on anything that he set his mind to. For Herb, he always took his struggles and used them as a learning experience. Being from Arkansas, he grew up around racism and many inequalities, but as he looked around growing up, he was also able to see the possibilities that surrounded him and the opportunities that were presented to him. He took the obstacles and challenges and looked at them through a different lens. He chose to see how he could overcome the challenges and not be held back by them, as he puts it, "often times it is those that do you wrong that you learn from the most."

In his town, they didn't have a lot of recreational sports, and it wasn't until he was 12 that he was actually able to play organized sports. His first official game he played was football, and at the first game, he ran all the way down the field for what he thought was a touchdown. He put the ball down thinking he had scored, a feeling of overwhelming excitement filled his body, but he was just short of the touchdown. It was an embarrassing moment for him, and he thought maybe he should try a different sport instead, but he did continue to play football throughout high school and didn't make that same mistake again.

It was his senior year in high school that he decided, with the help of his high school basketball coach and mentor, to focus completely on basketball. Herb always chose to listen to those people that told him what he can do and not what he can't do. Herb had a lot of natural athletic talent; however, he could not have gotten to where he did without a lot of work and a lot of practice athletically, but also getting good grades. To get to where he wanted to be he needed to make the choice that practicing and studying needed to come first.

Herb's mentor and coach always told him that he had seen so much talent get rejected from further pursuing their athletic dreams simply because they did not do well in the classroom. He chose to surround himself with others who had common goals like him, an error often by those who did not do well academically. He watched a lot of his friends get drawn into peer pressure and go down the wrong path, a choice he easily could have made.

His advice to youth and even adults who want to do better and be better, "if you want to achieve your goals and dreams, surround yourself with those who have the same goals and ambitions that you do." This is what he did from a young age. He and his friends wouldn't only compete on the court, but they would also compete in the classroom. The idea is to always strive to be a better version of yourself.

As a Harlem Globetrotter, he was also known as "Flight Time" for his incredible ability to jump. He became a world-renowned Harlem Globetrotter and played with them for 18 years. His nickname came from his coach Manny Jackson, owner of the Globetrotters when he first began. Manny thought every time Herb jumped, he should get frequent flyer miles, and this is where the name came from, and it stuck.

Herb realizes the pressures from society and social media that are put on youth today. He often tells young people, especially his own children, to not be pressured by what others want you to be. Research different interests and talk to your friends or family who are doing what you might want to do and learn how they got to be who they are today.

Each child is unique, and it is a parent's job to guide them not force them into doing what they want their child to do. He says this especially for those parents who were athletes and now want their child to live out the dreams that they as parents didn't. It's too much pressure, and youth ultimately lose the love of the game.

Herb attributes a lot of his ability to do what he has done in life to his mentors along the way. Today he believes that having the right mindset can make anything happen and become reality. Still as an adult, he continues to dream and set goals for himself. He instills this in his children and tries to set an example for other parents who may feel "their time has passed." He says that parents can be proud of what they did and share those stories with their children, but also, show them what you are doing now.

Today Herb is creating the life he wants every day and finding a way to do what he loves and serve his community. His hashtag and motto are *#kindnessisfree* because it doesn't cost anything to spread kindness wherever you go. Herbs book, *Projects, Popes and Presidents,* is meant to help youth believe they can do anything beyond their wildest dreams, just like he did.

42

5

Understanding Outside Influences:
What is normal anyways?

"Why fit in when you were born to stand out?" – Dr. Seuss

First, I am pleased to let you in on a little secret… there isn't any such thing as normal! Nothing is normal, and normal doesn't exist. Normal is a perception and what you think is normal may not be normal to other people. We often see this in different cultures. So often in the world today we are surrounded by what society tells us or what family tells us should or should not be. We must learn to look at the world in a way that is different and question what we are being told.

We are frequently pressured by expectations. For example, we must get better grades in school; we must go to college; we must know what we want to do or be as an adult at an early age. Many times, these expectations give us a feeling of anxiety, depression, or feeling overwhelmed, because we just don't know.

For myself at 43 years old, life has brought twists and turns, ups and downs and often, even when we feel we know why we do what we do or what our purpose is, we question it because we have setbacks in our mission and in our goals. Understanding that our world does not need to be nor look like what the outside world calls "normal" is key when making decisions in our life.

Growing up I was often told that to do well in life, you need to get a good paying job, you need to be a doctor, lawyer, pharmacist, etc., and none of those things were attractive to me. So, when you are looking at your talents, your interests, what you want to do with your life, there is no cookie cutter image or vision to what that needs to look like. Looking around at the world, wanting to be like someone else, thinking that you need to conform with what others tell you, with what society tells you, is not true. In order to break from this cycle of having others dictate what you can or cannot do or what you should or should not be, you have to be strong and unwavering in your desires and dreams.

Being unwavering and strong can be challenging. It might mean upsetting family members. It might mean not listening to a guidance counselor. It might mean going against what someone tells you that you cannot do. If you look throughout history at the many people who have had success in their lives, many of these people's stories right here in this book, you can see that they went against what other people told them. However, it's not easy when loved ones, people that you confide in, people with whom you trust, tell you that your desire or goal is impossible.

What people tell us we can't do, such as parents, teachers, guidance counselors, government officials, and so on, really is their own opinion or perspective based on how they were raised or what society has told them thus far. Often, we grow up having acquired these same thoughts and ideals which create who we are and what we project onto the world around us. We cannot allow someone else's perceptions and pre-conditioned thoughts change the course of our life.

I have been told many times that what I am trying to do myself, in changing the education system, is a stupid idea and will never be done. It's wishful thinking. It's a poor investment. No one will ever invest in that. Then I took the advice of a wonderful man, Greg Reid, which was to just smile and say, "Thank you very much. I will take that into consideration." I don't argue with them; I don't get depressed or allow them to change my mind. It is their opinion, and whether I choose to take it or leave it is my prerogative.

Sometimes other people only know what they know. They have never seen a change, a large change in the education system in their lifetime. Therefore, to them, it is something that seems impossible. However, I cannot allow one person, no matter if they're my next-door neighbor or an influential, wealthy, well-known man or woman, to allow me to question what I am doing, especially when I know I am on the course of life meant for me.

Now I will not lie and say that I am not taken aback when someone tells me it's impossible. I will not lie and say that in the moment, I don't want to breakdown and cry, because it's not easy when someone tells you that you are not going to accomplish what you are trying to accomplish, and this is where your confidence, your strength, and your belief in yourself truly comes in. Always remember, just because someone else can't do it, doesn't mean that you can't do it!

When people tell me something is impossible, I always refer to what Naveen Jain said to me, "if people don't think you're crazy, if people don't tell you that you can't do it, then you're not thinking big enough," and that puts me back into the mindset I need to be in. So, it is very difficult when people literally stomp on something that you are really excited about, but you have to let that go. Don't waver if you truly feel inside that it's what you are meant to be doing.

When you are looking to do something so big or even something small, there are always going to be people around you that are going to tell you that you can't either, because no one has ever done it, because they themselves can't do it, or because they don't want to see success in your life. Therefore, it is so important to surround yourself with like-minded people who have the desire and the obsession to accomplish their goals and dreams.

We must remember we are a multicultural society, and beliefs and values are globally different. Certain Middle Eastern countries believe that women are beneath men. Is that true? Absolutely not, or at least not in the society that most modern-day people live in. So even looking at just this small example is proof that it all depends on what people consider from their own point of view to be normal. I'm here to tell you today there is no normal. Your core values and your core beliefs are normal only if you are living a life of honesty and integrity. That is normal.

Now many would say opposite of that because we live in a world with massive corruption. We live in a world that looks to doing the wrong thing or making the wrong choices excusable because they make it look like it was "necessary" in order to get there. It is never necessary to be corrupt or dishonest in order to achieve your goals. It is never necessary to make someone else hurt, to put them down or feel ashamed for who they are, to further your goals. That is not normal. However, people make excuses for that all the time, outside influences, especially if there are people that you hold in high regard, will make you question your value system, your ethics, and your need to remember who you are and what you want out of your life.

At the end of the day whether or not anybody else knows what you did or did not do, you have to ultimately look yourself in the mirror and know what you did, and sometimes people don't have a conscience and don't think there's anything wrong with it. Then you get a little bit further and do something else, and a little bit further, and do something else and then, your integrity and your ethics are exchanged with dishonesty and corruption.

So, it is really hard in the world that we live in to keep our inner beliefs and our inner values aligned with who we want to be. It is really hard to turn off the outside world and follow our own path to what we want, when there are always naysayers and always people going up against us, but the harder it is, the better the path, because nothing in this life, nothing that anybody in the past has accomplished, no one who has true ethical success and values in their life has accomplished it without obstacles.

Now let's look at some historical figures who we can learn more about, from different cultures, who did not conform and go with the normal of the societal world they lived in. First are Martin Luther King Jr., John Lewis, and Rosa Parks, and all of the men and women of the civil rights movement. These people had the vision of a new world, an equal world. They did it in a way of peace and love, a way that many of us today look at in amazement. They were the vision of integrity, of obsession and desire to make a better world for themselves and for their children and for all the people who suffered before them, that their losses and their sacrifices weren't in vain. People told them they would not be able to do it. People told them that they were crazy to think that anything was going to change. These are the people who need to be inspiring you; they're who inspire me; they're who I think about when someone tells me I will never change what I want to change in this world.

Next is Nelson Mandela, the great president of South Africa who was jailed for 27 years because he fought against Apartheid. If at the beginning of his mission he would have given up, if he was not the leader that the people needed, then it would have been someone else eventually. That's what you need to remember. That you are not the only one who dreams big or wants to change the world. What you need to remember is that if you don't do it, someone else will, and who knows how many more years it would have taken for apartheid to leave South Africa. Here is a man who was jailed for many years, imprisoned for fighting the system. I don't know if I could have done it. I will be honest. That is strength; that is courage; that is a mission. He went against the normal of what his society, of what his world around him was telling him was supposed to be normal. If there is injustice, cruelty, corruption, and dishonesty, that is never normal and that can always be changed. He was living proof of that as well.

There are many others who have paved the way for you and me to believe and dream big. Margaret Thatcher, the first female prime minister of Great Britain. Malala, a teenage girl who started speaking out at a young age on behalf of girls' rights to an education in Pakistan, which made her a target for the Taliban and was shot in the head. However, she survived, and continued to be an activist and later won the Nobel Peace Prize!

Gandhi was able to mass hundreds of thousands of people to create a movement of peace. Passively! What he did was extraordinary. He brought people from fighting factions together to create peace and love throughout his country.

Jesus… no matter if you are Christian or not, you cannot deny that this man lived, was a servant of God and that his way of the world was in humility and equality for everyone. He was a teacher who guided people to peace and love and have faith to believe in themselves, to believe in God, and he did not just say it, he showed it. He showed love; he showed empathy; he showed compassion, he showed humility, in a very corrupt world, and he too had to be sacrificed for his desire to create a more loving and better world. They all suffered, and they all made sacrifices for the better of the whole.

These are all individuals. So today when someone tells you, you can't do it; you're just one person; don't believe it. Everything depends on how much you want it. One small act changes the world for a great many people and one stance can make a difference.

So, I ask you now, can you define normal? Because I can't. Everyone is a unique individual. What other people want for their life will be different than what you want for your life, and that's great. You show support and don't put down their dreams. There is no normal. There is no box that we need to all fit into. Live the life that you want to live. Dream the dreams that you want to dream. Be the person that you want to be. As the naysayers. negative people or haters come and go, especially when you're down, it just means that you must be doing something right. Make your mark no matter how big or how small, only you know what normal is for you.

The Story of Mike Poglese
The Pressures of Outside Influence

"If the system fails you, then create your own." – Mike Poglese

At such a young age, Mike Poglese has had his share of ups and downs. From selling drugs in high school to having his first taste of success at 21, he is now in his late 20's and the co-founder of more than one company. However, his road to this moment was one built with many pitfalls, and could have made anyone want to give up, but for Mike, the setbacks were truly setups. He has learned and grown from every one of them. What he realized is that every setback in his life has literally been a set up for a tremendous breakthrough.

Mike Poglese was born outside of Lansing, Michigan. His parents had him young; his mom was 16 and his dad was 18. They separated early after Mike was born as his dad at this time lived in a trailer and was selling weed, and his mom needed to be responsible to take care of Mike. So, she decided to leave Michigan and move to Richmond, Virginia to live with their great-aunt.

As a child, Mike remembers being passed around a lot as he was the central focus of being in and out of courtrooms as his parents fought for custody. He had to move from state to state because of the desire for custody on both sides, and he saw it as being lucky because most dads probably wouldn't have cared, but his dad wanted to stay in his life. His dad never gave up on him.

During his childhood, his mom was working full time and going to college. Often, he would go with his mom to class and work on snow days because she didn't have anyone to watch him. His mom worked hard to do everything she could to support him.

Although he did a lot of extracurricular activities, he was lost as a teen, and he turned to drugs and alcohol. It started at 14 with chewing tobacco, and one day when he was hanging out with his friends at the park, someone said they had marijuana, and they went to smoke it in the tunnels by the pond. It was an instant, a moment, where his life completely changed because of this one choice he made.

Reflecting back now, that moment was the catalyst to the downturn into selling drugs. Mike knows that had he not been hanging out with these people on this day, he wouldn't have started getting involved with drugs. However, another reason it was so attractive was because he didn't have a job; he didn't have any money, and his mom didn't make enough at the time for him to do other things with his friends that he wanted to do.

This is where young people, who don't have financial means to do what they want, get themselves into trouble, because as soon as the money starts to come in, and you aren't limited anymore in what you can do, it becomes more and more attractive. He knew though that he would have to get a job in order to buy what he wanted because if not his mother would wonder how he was getting all of the new things he had or even why he wasn't hungry, because now he could always eat out with his friends. Therefore, to hide what he was really doing, he got a job at a golf course.

Mike had a lot of close calls with the law. It wasn't just easy money. He often got pulled over, but luckily for him, he didn't get caught. He was selling drugs, drinking, and not surrounding himself with the right people. Mike put little effort into high school, and even more so when he was being pressured by those around him to get good grades to go to college. He just didn't care, and he didn't see the value at the time.

Mike made it through high school, and one of the reasons he chose to go to college farther away from home was to get out of that environment, because deep inside he knew that if he kept it up, something bad was going to happen. He attended Coastal Carolina University. Although he wanted to get away from the troubles, he had created for himself in Richmond, his school choice was not one based on academics. It was a choice based on being the number one-party school at the time, and because he loved the water, he wanted to live on the beach and possibly study Marine Biology.

The first semester however, like many young people who first go off to college, was one of fun but also one of trouble. On his first night, he got an alcohol ticket at an off-campus party for drinking outside, and before the end of the semester, he got a second write-up. He ended up getting arrested at the end of the semester with a possession charge and was suspended. Not a good start to doing better by putting himself in similar situations as he did before.

During his suspension, Mike went back home and worked at a golf course for 6 months. It was then that he realized he got really lucky and that it hadn't been worse. It was at this point where he also realized he wasn't invisible, and one day he was going to end up with serious and irreversible charges. Eventually, he returned to school. He stayed out of trouble and managed to make it to the last semester of his senior year when unexpectedly another setback came along. This time he did nothing wrong other than being guilty by association.

Mike's roommates got caught for possession of drugs, and although Mike was not involved and was not charged with anything, the school considered it his third write-up. Even though he proved he was not connected in any way, and he was never charged; he was still expelled during his last semester right before graduation. This was difficult for Mike to accept at the time, but after the fact, he realized that everything happens for a reason, and without this happening, he would not be where he is today.

Now Mike is an entrepreneur. He runs his own business and has created success despite the early events of his life. His thoughts for young people today, "Don't get lost; figure out who you really want to be. Get someone to help you with the right mindset; live your life with purpose and intent, and things will start to flow together for you. Be clear on what you want in life. Don't live your life for others, live it for yourself. Make your own choices, not what society wants or what your parents want. If the system fails you, then create your own."

6

Indifference

"The world will not be destroyed by those who do evil, but by those who watch them without doing anything." – Albert Einstein

Have you ever stood by and watched something happen that you knew you could possibly help the situation, but did nothing? I think it is fair to say that we all have. Indifference is standing by and watching things around you happening and not doing much about them. You don't feel one way or another. You have no real interest in liking it or disliking it. There's no enthusiasm, no real concern. It's neither good nor bad.

When we look around the world, and we see how the world is today, there are a lot of people who are indifferent, young and old. Often people don't get involved or people don't do anything about situations until it affects them personally. Many people go through life just saying things like, "Poverty, yeah it's really too bad," but they're not poor. They know it exists, but they choose to do nothing about it or do something to help the situation. The same with teen trafficking, which happens very often. When you choose to turn a blind eye and do nothing about it, you are being indifferent.

A simple example we can all relate to is bullying. Have you ever watched someone get bullied and not do anything about it, even if it's just to tell someone else who might be able to help? Perhaps you were bullied, and someone was there and saw, but that person didn't say or do anything. I think we all have turned away in different situations, at one time or another when we could have helped.

You may be thinking, "What can I really do; I'm only one person?" Let's recall the great examples that all started with one small act. Imagine if Martin Luther King Jr. were indifferent about civil rights. It was happening to him as well, but imagine if he decided that he wasn't going to take action; he was going to be submissive and allow people to treat him the way they treated everyone, and he said, "Well what can I really do about it? I'm only one person."

If you don't know who Rosa Parks is, she is the African American woman who chose to sit at the front of the bus as opposed to the back of the bus where African Americans were "supposed" to sit. She was only one person, but her one action to show this wasn't fair let her voice be known without saying a word.

Imagine if Gandhi didn't care to help others and find peace in the world. With his few small acts, step-by-step, he created an incredible movement for peace and nonviolence.

Nelson Mandela and the steps he took being in jail for all those years because he used his voice at a time where he was supposed to stay silent. If he stayed silent, then South Africa would not have seen the drastic changes to eradicate Apartheid, and he would never have become the first black president of the country.

These are incredible and inspirational people to show that one small step toward something greater, something better, something against evil, does make a difference. It's interesting how many things have been accomplished in this world because of people taking action and not sitting by and being indifferent or complacent.

Now let's look at indifference in the realm of social media. We often see people doing or saying things they shouldn't. We also see people using social media for a cause or to raise awareness for the greater good. Just like most things in the world there is a good side and a bad side. Do you use social media to express your thoughts and opinions about something you care about? If you see someone being bullied on social media, do you reach out or tell someone? What do you do if you see someone posting things that may signal signs of depression or sadness? If you know there is a way you can help someone and show kindness, then do it. It is not about being Gandhi, Nelson Mandela, Rosa Parks, or anyone else for that matter. For them it began with one small act towards a cause they believed in. One small step of not being indifferent and not ignoring something around them that they didn't like.

Lastly but just as important, there is indifference to your success. This is when many people pass through life by saying, "Well, it just wasn't meant for me. This is what it is. I tried once but it didn't work out. I'll just work for now because college just isn't for me." Let me put it this way, you were not created to just be good or get by. You are meant to thrive. We all are.

There were many times I just went with what I knew, with what was comfortable. Now I have been an educator for over 20 years. Imagine how many times I could have said, "My students don't care, so I don't care. They want to fail. I'll let them fail." This happens so often, where parents can't be bothered, teachers can't be bothered, friends can't be bothered, all because some people just think it's someone else's responsibility.

It's your life and being indifferent, just going with the flow, and not really caring for what's happening in the world around you is not why you were put on this Earth. You don't need to start a movement, but it might be that one word, that one talk with a friend who is having a difficult time, that one act when you see somebody that's struggling or being bullied, that you go and say, 'I'm here for you.' Stand for what you believe in;

you will feel better, and you will make the world a better place as well.

The Story of
Altagracia Pierre-Outerbridge
Challenge Yourself to Be Your Best

"Desire, determination, and perseverance; if you really want what you want, you can do anything." – Altagracia Pierre-Outerbridge

The life of Altagracia Pierre-Outerbridge did not start as one faced with challenges and struggles. She describes her childhood as relatively average. Born and raised in Haiti, she grew up speaking French in a fairly wealthy family. As a child, she lived comfortably, but being one of six children, she often felt unseen, invisible. She describes her childhood self as being plain, nothing remarkable or special.

Throughout her life Altagracia has always challenged herself and done well in school to compensate for not being seen or heard as a person or taken seriously as a woman of color. With her father who would constantly read and learn, Altagracia knew that she could make people notice her if she could speak well and present herself in a way that people would want to listen.

Altagracia's father was very ill as she grew up and her brother was assassinated one night when she was 15, which was when her life changed. In fear that the same people who killed her brother would come for the whole family, her parents sent the kids to settle in different places before they themselves looked for safety. It wasn't easy to find a place for them to go. While some fled to the Dominican Republic, Altagracia, with her 12-year-old brother, was sent to New York on a plane alone until her mother could later join them. Her mother came about a year later, and her father passed away.

When Altagracia and her brother arrived in the United States, they stayed with her mother's cousin, who played a very important role in Altagracia's life. She was a woman who had great strength and courage, and to this day when Altagracia struggles with life, she just remembers her "aunt" and thinks of her strength.

Upon arriving in the United States Altagracia needed to learn English if she wanted to do well in school. She needed to start over, and she continuously pushed herself to be the best she could be. She joined Model UN where she actually had to speak in front of people, and while she knew what she was saying, she didn't understand the majority of what everyone else was saying. However, being native in French, she pushed herself and was able to pick up quickly, as many of the root words were similar and ultimately, she won awards. She then decided to take AP classes and did better than most native speakers on the SAT. She attributes her internal drive and love for learning to her father, whom she calls an intellectual and a "Renaissance" man.

Altagracia knew that in order to make a good life for herself, she had to call upon the intelligence she knew she had. In 12th grade, Manhattan College had a scholarship test for students who wanted to study languages. She never thought she would be able to go to college because her mom couldn't afford it, and she knew if she wanted to go it would only be through her sheer will and determination. Because she didn't even have the money to take the test, two of her teachers paid the fees for her, and she received a call from the foreign language department at the college offering her a scholarship. Unfortunately, even after the scholarship money, she would still be responsible for paying a lot more than she could afford, and the college ended up offering to pay for everything.

One could call it serendipity or the universe aligning with the way things continued to go for Altagracia or perhaps it was God's plan. There was another struggle at this time that she needed to overcome and that was her 2-hour commute to and from campus each day. It was difficult and didn't allow her to enjoy herself or really meet new people. So, one day her professor told her about a position as resident advisor which would allow her to live on campus and pay for her books. She applied and got the position. For Altagracia, her hard work and dedication really paid off in providing her opportunities that she never would have had.

Mentors are the key to everything. "When you put your best foot forward, people will come in your path and guide you the right way and the right doors open miraculously." After she graduated from college, she spent a year working as a waitress. A professor then called her and told her she should apply to law school. She was accepted and continued working as a waitress through law school and even after her bar exam while getting her MBA. With all of this said and done, this was not an easy road for Altagracia, as she did all of this while working on getting her legal paperwork to be in the United States, and this was another challenge she struggled with every day.

Fast forward 10 years as a lawyer, working extremely long hours already and looking for a new challenge, Altagracia decided to open her own law firm, and not just anywhere, she decided to open it in one of the most competitive areas she could think of, Midtown Manhattan. Everyone thinking she was crazy, not only for the location, nor simply because she was a woman, but she was a woman of color. She can say it was challenging; however, she now smiles as two years have gone by, and her law firm continues to grow and be successful with 26 employees and contractors. It's inspiring to say the least! Her lesson to young people, especially young immigrants who are struggling to make a better life for themselves, "Desire, hard work, and perseverance; if you really want what you want, you can do anything."

7

Gratitude

"Let us rise up and be thankful, for if we didn't learn a lot today, at least we learned a little, and if we didn't learn a little, at least we didn't get sick, and if we got sick, at least we didn't die; so, let us all be thankful." – Buddha

Gratitude is the quality of being thankful; readiness to show appreciation for and to return kindness. When we can show gratitude for what we have, we will open our minds to seeing how fortunate we really are. No matter what your circumstances are today, I am sure you can look around and find those that are less fortunate than you. I never start a day without recognizing 10 things that I am grateful for, and I never end a day without reflecting on what happened that day to say thank you!

There are a great many books on gratitude. I challenge you each day to look around you and find 10 things you are grateful for because we take so much for granted. You might be looking at your current circumstances and saying, "how can I possibly make a list of 10 things I am grateful for every day?" In the beginning, I thought the same thing, but the more you think about it and the more you learn about the world around you, the more you will realize you have more to be thankful for than you thought.

Let me give you an example. Here is a list of ten things off the top of my head that you might be grateful for which are probably the first and most generic things that come to mind, such as:
    1. – food
    2. – clothing
    3. – your home

4. – family
5. – school
6. – friends
7. – your phone
8. – pet
9. – your computer
10. – your health

You may even struggle to get these first 10 things, but let's dig deeper.

First, let's look at food. Perhaps you can eat any food without causing discomfort within your body, meaning you don't have food allergies or certain ailments towards food. Do you have a constant flow of food options in your refrigerator or have the ability to eat out when you want to? That is something else to be grateful for.

How about clean water? Do you have clean water to drink every day? I know that in the United States and Canada, you can open the faucet and drink right from there in most places, and when I am in the US, I say thank you every time I do. Imagine, there are people in the world without running water in their house. I know that living in the Dominican Republic, many places don't have indoor plumbing, and you would have to fill a bucket and poor it down the toilet in order to flush. As well, many people in many countries depend on rainwater or an outdoor hose to fill buckets and barrels to take a shower, and until I went to a place like this and experienced it myself, it was something that I often took for granted. Now, every time I take a hot shower, I cannot help but be grateful and thank God that I am fortunate enough to have hot water.

Another scenario is when I first moved to the Dominican Republic, I did not have a regular washing machine that you put the clothes in, turn it on and then go back 30 minutes later, and it was done. It was "semi-automatic." You had to fill the machine with a hose, then turn it on to wash, then drain it, and then take the clothes out and put them in a centrifuge to spin and wring the water out. Imagine that! It sure made me much more grateful for the automatic washer and dryer back home.

We take so many of the little things in life for granted, and we often focus on what we don't have instead of what we do have. I will assure you that if you are reading this book, you can be grateful that you have the ability to read. You are educated. You probably go to school or have gone to school. There are many children that never get the opportunity to attend school. Hopefully, by now, your mind has started to shift, and a great many other things have come into your mind about what you can be thankful for. Here are a few more.

Electricity, without it, you wouldn't have internet, a way to charge your phone, keep the food in your refrigerator from spoiling, watch T.V., use your blow-dryer or hair straightener, and that water that comes out of your faucet or is hot when you want it to be, all thanks to electricity. How about your toothbrush and toothpaste, soap, the chair you are sitting on while reading this book, your bed, the door to your room or to your house, windows to keep the bugs and mosquitoes out, and the list will go on and on.

So, why am I diving so deeply into gratitude? Because we tend to be "I wish I had…" people. As was stated before, we often wish we had what others have, and when we can get out of our own way and be grateful for what we do have and stop focusing on what we don't have, we will then start to feel greater joy and happiness in our own lives. We often look on social media and see the things that other people have and want their life; we often overlook what is truly behind it all. Things don't bring happiness. However, I can guarantee that gratitude for what you do have will bring you joy in this very moment.

Now, I want you to try this, and I challenge you for the next 7 days to actually write down every morning 10 things you are grateful for, and every night, 10 things that you are grateful for that happened that day before you go to bed, without repeating anything. As well, do one act of kindness each day. For example, I was listening to a woman speak about a difficult time that she is going through, and I reached out to her on Instagram and just told her that she is in my thoughts and prayers. I don't know her, but she was grateful and said thank you. I wasn't expecting anything in return, but I am sure it helped her in some small way.

Yesterday, a friend sent me a 10 second message telling me that he and his team were there to listen and help in whatever challenges I may be facing, and that was his act of kindness to me. It made me feel wonderful, and it was one of the things on my gratitude list last night. So, I challenge you to do the same, and in 7 days, you will see how it is changing your life, even if it is in just a small way.

The Story of Naveen Jain
A Life to Be Grateful For

"Dream so big that people think you are crazy and never be afraid to fail because you only fail when you give up. Everything else is just a learning experience." - Naveen Jain

Naveen Jain is an inspiration to anyone who has had the opportunity to listen to him and knowing his story and the journey to get to be where he is today will truly make you believe you can too. He points out to young people today that it is easier to create success now than when he started out because of technology and the ability to immediately be connected with anyone, anywhere. When Naveen began his journey the only way to connect with someone or learn from them was to go to them physically or somehow find their phone number to speak with them; not an easy task and quite expensive to do.

When Naveen was 10, he watched America put a man on the moon. This meant everything to him, and he thought that someday it would be possible for this village boy to be successful if he could just get to America. In that moment, he decided he was going to do everything he could to be a part of the American dream. He did not allow anyone or anything change his mind. This was difficult to do when growing up surrounded by poverty and people who lived with a scarcity mindset, but the young boy didn't allow anything alter what he knew deep within; he believed in himself.

Naveen was born in India. He grew up in the worst poverty you can imagine. Yet through grit and determination, he managed to earn an engineering degree and an MBA before emigrating to the United States at the age of 22— arriving with just $5 in his pocket and a very limited English vocabulary. However, when he reached his goal and made it to America in

1982, Naveen almost changed his mind and went back to India. He arrived in Flemington, New Jersey rented an old farmhouse along with six other people, sharing a $500 "beater of a car." He found a minimum wage job, and life was great, or at least he thought it was, because coming from an Indian slum to such "lavish" living was something he actually never could have imagined. However, what he wasn't expecting and had never experienced before was winter.

Quoted from his bestselling book Moonshots, he states, "Then October came, and the snow began to fall. And fall. Snow was an utterly new experience for me, and I was not prepared for it. I had no warm clothes or boots, and the only shoes I did have had holes in them. Suddenly India wasn't looking so bad. I was actually thinking of going back home when I met a man who was working at Burroughs (now Unisys). When I told him of my plans, he pleaded with me to reconsider, suggesting that I go to Silicon Valley instead. "You're a bright guy," he told me. "We could really use you in this country. You've got talent. Let me make a few calls and set up a few interviews for you—I know you'll succeed there." And with that, I did indeed make the move to Silicon Valley and grew into a wonderful career in technology."

Had this man not crossed Naveen's path at a time when he needed it most, he may have gone back to India, and the man we know today may have never existed. Call it Divine Intervention, call it Serendipity or the Law of Attraction, Naveen was meant for bigger and better things than going back to India. In time, he landed a job at Microsoft, where his work on Windows 95 earned him both patents and accolades for his standout program management work. From there, he ventured and founded InfoSpace, which became one of the largest internet businesses in America. He then went on to be the founder of a series of other companies, including, Intelius, TalentWise, Moon Express and Viome. Along the way, he was awarded the Albert Einstein Technology Medal, named one of the "Most Creative People in Business" by Fast Company, and was presented the Ellis Island Medal of Honor. Today, with Moon Express, he is in the process of opening a new era of lunar exploration dedicated to solving the world's energy problems. Impossible as it seems, this is his story, and he believes if he can do something like this, anyone can.

Naveen's family didn't have to be poor, but it was his father's choice because he preferred honesty over corruption. His dad had a good job in the government as a civil engineer responsible for the construction of government buildings, but he could not be bribed. India is an extremely corrupt society, as are many countries, and his dad, in his humble wisdom, decided that he wanted to be an honest man. Therefore, the family was moved from place to place, because his father couldn't be paid off by people to get what they wanted. Naveen's family would get transferred to the most rural areas, and his education would come in places where there weren't any tables, chairs, or chalkboards; you sat on the floor and wrote on the floor.

Despite the struggles faced by his family, he attributes much of his success in life to his ability to overcome the adversities he faced as a child, and he is grateful to have been raised the way he was by his parents. He is grateful that they instilled in him the values of trust, integrity, and honesty, and that these values were never to be compromised no matter the situation or circumstances. Even with the lack of educational opportunities as a child, education was the focus to changing his future and the future of his siblings.

So, what exactly was his motivation to create all these companies and have such incredibly bold, and what some might call crazy, visions? It was his desire to help solve the world's greatest problems and help as many people as he could by doing so. Naveen has decided that it is his mission to take on the world's greatest issues with the companies he has created to make the world a better place. He is not afraid to fail, as he knows life is eternally filled with ups and downs. He often tells young people that this is how you know you are alive. When you think of a heartbeat and look at a heart monitor, it goes up and down. If you are looking to live a stable life, a smooth life, you are choosing not to be alive at all.

Naveen has founded many companies over the years, some successful, others still in progress, but Naveen has always been very aware throughout his life that there would be times that things would not go the way they were planned. However, he did not allow those moments to hold him back from having even bigger and bolder dreams. For Naveen it is what you learn along the way that provides the support necessary to go for the moonshots!

Today, Naveen continues to be an entrepreneur and philanthropist driven to solve the world's biggest challenges through innovation. He is now on a mission to make illness optional with his company Viome which studies gut biology to give you insights on your unique biology and microbiome as well as recommend the right foods for you to eat to stay healthy. Although he has gone from five dollars in his pocket to extreme wealth, he is truly humble and has instilled such humility in his children. He says, "Humility is a sure sign of knowing when somebody has been successful. Because when you still have an iota of arrogance left in you, then you're still trying to prove something to yourself or someone else. That means you're still not successful."

8

<u>Responsibility</u>

Accept responsibility for your life. Know that it is you who will get you where you want to go, no one else. - Les Brown

Responsibility in today's world, even on the smallest level, seems to be lacking in a tremendous way. I see this most in young people that I have worked with throughout the years, and the trend seems to be getting worse instead of better. Unfortunately, we live in a world where making excuses is accepted and where parents allow their children to get away with being irresponsible, by making excuses themselves. You may remember a time when you chose not to study for an important test or left an assignment until the last minute, knowing you would fail or not receive a good grade. However, you still decided not to be responsible and chose not to do it. Why?

A lot of times it is because in the back of our mind we know that there is some way to get out of having to do it in that moment, there is someone else we can blame it on, or your mom or dad will advocate for you to give you another chance. Why should you have another chance when you consciously chose not to do the responsible thing which would have been to study for the test or do the assignment. Do you think your parents are helping you by swooping in to save the day for your lack of responsibility? Absolutely not, and parents that are doing this are sending a clear message to their child that they don't need to be responsible.

When a parent does this for a child, it does much more harm than good. First, you are being taught that if you choose to be irresponsible, then there aren't any consequences. While not studying for a test or doing an assignment may not seem

71

overly detrimental in the long-term, imagine if that were a task your boss asked you to accomplish at work, and you decided you didn't feel like doing it. Are you going to bring your mom and dad to work to explain why you didn't complete it on time? No, of course not. Your boss is going to fire you, and then you will most likely make an excuse and put the blame on your boss or someone else, because in your mind, it couldn't possibly be your fault.

Technically, if you have never been held accountable or needed to be responsible for your actions because someone always came in and saved the day, then in reality, it is not completely your fault. However, the day is going to come where you will have a very rude awakening for your lack of responsibility, and hopefully by reading this you will understand. Let's use an example:

You have a job interview tomorrow for a summer internship at a place you would really love to work, let's say Google. However, the night before your friend has a big party, and you have 'FOMO,' if you aren't there for the entire time. Your interview is at 8 o'clock in the morning, and in your mind, you know what you should do (go home early and get ready for the interview.) However, the little voice in your head comes out and thinks of all the viable excuses you can make to reschedule the interview and be able to stay at the party until the end.

So, you choose to be irresponsible because you think someone else will "bail you out." The next day comes, you miss the interview, you have your mom or dad call to tell them you are sick, and you have to reschedule the interview… maybe, or maybe not!

That morning your mom comes to you and says she called, and they were sorry to hear that you are not well, but today is the only day for interviews, and there are no other available appointments. The ship has sailed. You lost a great opportunity. However, in your mind, you are searching to shift the blame on someone else. You say, "How can they do that? What if I really was sick? That wouldn't be fair," or you say to your parents, "Why didn't you make me come home? You knew how important this was," or you say to yourself, "It's not my fault. I am a teenager. I am supposed to have fun and enjoy life. I shouldn't have to be pressured to make such a choice." The list goes on and on.

While this might be the path you are meant to travel and forgoing this position at Google possibly will open a different or better door for you, you cannot know this at the time. Being responsible is not making excuses or shifting the blame on anyone else but yourself. If your alarm doesn't go off, and you are late for school, it's your fault for not having a back-up plan. If you are running late and missed the bus, it's your fault for not getting up earlier to ensure you had enough time to be on time. If you are finding a class difficult, don't like the teacher, and are failing, it's your fault, because in life, nothing is easy, you won't like everyone, and you have to find a way to be your best no matter what the circumstances may be.

Lack of responsibility and feeling there aren't any consequences when it comes to being irresponsible is a major issue today for youth and adults. Ultimately, you have control of your life, and your choices dictate what will happen. Being late, not doing the work, making excuses, all these things are within your control. So, the next time you are mad at your parents because you need something for a project and waited until the last day to start it, that is entirely on you. There is no one to blame for what happens to you but yourself.

I will leave you with one last example. A young boy had been talking with his friend during class, and after several warnings, they both got detention. When the boy got home and told his mother about what happened, the next day she came to school to have a meeting. The situation was explained to her, but she just kept saying, "my son said the other boy wouldn't stop talking to him, and he was not to blame." The teacher simply stated, "if that were the case, then your son could have ignored him, or told me, and I would have moved him. However, he chose to continue after multiple warnings to stop."

Do you see where I am going with this? It is one excuse after another, and the mother is only teaching her child that he can do whatever he wants without any repercussions, but the day will come when she is not there, he will expect to get away with something, and he won't know what to do. As well, this meeting was a waste of time for the teacher, the parent, and the child, all so the child could be right in a situation where he made the wrong choice.

Now let's look at being responsible on social media. We are bombarded every second with incredible amounts of information. We post, share, like and tweet all day long sometimes. What are the advantages and disadvantages, and where does responsibility come into play with social media? While it is fun to Facetime and Snap Chat with our friends, I guarantee that the majority of you have been distracted and put something off that needed to be done because you were too busy "playing" on social media. How about saying something negative or messaging someone something that was unkind or hurtful, perhaps with the excuse that they did it or said it first.

While all these Apps can be fun and keep us connected, let us remember that what we post, share and how we portray ourselves is now out there for the whole world to see. Sometimes even after you erase something, it can still be found, so think about it before you write or send anything. Ask yourself, "Will this make me a better person? Does it benefit me or my friends in any way?" Recently young people who have sent naked or sexy photos of themselves have gotten into a lot of trouble with the law, even arrested, as it is considered sending child pornography. If you are charged with it, that will stay with you for the rest of your life, so think before you act, because there are some things that no one, no matter who they are, can erase in the end.

Responsibility and more so, the lack of responsibility people show, is the #1 reason why most young people and adults do not succeed in life. They feel entitled, that it is always someone else's fault, and they are never to blame. So, I ask that the next time you blame someone or something else for what is happening or has happened in your life, be honest with yourself, and point the finger where it really belongs.

<u>The Story of Dr. Ana Olivero</u>
<u>Being Responsible for The Path You Take</u>

"Sometimes your parents will not support your choices; they will even tell you it's not possible because they don't think you have what it takes. Don't let this hold you back. When my father doubted my ability to be a doctor, it just made me want to do it even more, just to prove him wrong, and I did. I am actually grateful for his disbelief and lack of confidence in me, because it pushed me to prove him wrong and be who I am today." – Dr. Ana Olivero

The following story is one that may not be often heard of when thinking of growing up. We often hear of challenges like poverty, hunger, abuse, homelessness, however this next story is one of being a child caught in the middle of two political parties and living in fear that her uncles and mother would end up in jail, or even worse, dead.

Dr. Ana Olivero was born in a beautiful part of the Dominican Republic, Barahona, in a small town called Tamayo. She has fond memories of watering the roses, sitting for coffee in the afternoon with the neighbors and the love that she received from her family. However, her childhood would be a tumultuous one as she was also part of a family divided by political views and ideology that shaped her life forever.

Ana's grandmother had many children, and she instilled in her children that they be educated. Her two eldest uncles had university degrees. One was an engineer and the other was completing his studies as an anesthesiologist. These two men were a great hope for Ana's family. One of them was the first person to own a car in the little town she grew up in. She remembers how everyone would run to the windows when he drove by because they had never seen a car before. However, civil war came to the Dominican Republic, and her two uncles disappeared traveling back home from Santo Domingo to Tamayo never to be seen or heard from again.

After the civil war when Ana was around the age of five, she moved to Santo Domingo with her mother, aunt, uncles and her two cousins, who were orphans, after their father disappeared. Ana's parents were divorced, and so her mother took it upon herself to be the provider of the family to bring a better life and more opportunities to them. Her mother worked two jobs and studied at the same time as she had the dream to become a teacher, which she accomplished.

Ana grew up going to school with her sister and cousins, and she loved to learn. Ana's uncles, Manuel and Plinio Matos Moquete, were older and valued education as well, but they had very strong political views which ultimately put them and Ana's family at risk of being persecuted. These two men were great political figures, however, not as allies of the government, but as opposition to the government that existed. They were fighting for democracy.

As a child, Ana remembers growing up with a lot of persecution and political conflict. Often police would come to their house armed looking for her uncles at different times over the years. However, Ana was divided in the middle of everything that was happening, because while her uncles were on one side of the political views in favor of democracy, her father, Juan Esteban Olivero Feliz, was one of the predominant political figures on the other side, as President of the Senate under Joaquin Balaguer.

Ana attributes the resilience, strength, and courage she has today to her childhood. Watching the perseverance of her uncles continue their education after being incarcerated and one of them winning the Nobel Peace Prize in Literature made her realize that no matter what challenges you face in life or how difficult the situation is you can still accomplish anything you put your mind to. As well, she watched how her uncles never fell into the corrupt political system and never fell into the money and greed of the government even after the country becoming a democracy.

Because of her father's political position in the government, Ana was able to go to a private school as a teen. However, Ana did not make the right choices and acted out. She was facing the fear of her mother being incarcerated and her uncles possibly being killed. This was very stressful in Ana's life. She was not getting good grades, and she was expelled from attending the private school. Therefore, she had to attend a public school her senior year of high school, and for Ana, attending public school was the best experience of her life. She found a new path and direction for her life.

Ana knew from a young age she wanted to go into medicine. After she graduated high school, she went to see her father to tell him she was going to be a doctor, and she says that his response fueled her desire even further. He told her that she would never be a doctor, so she took on the challenge to prove him wrong, and she did.

Ana continued to fight and never gave up when presented different opportunities. She studied at the university in Santo Domingo. She could not afford much, and her mother could not afford more than two books. Her father didn't financially help her. Because her mother was the sister of political fugitives, she was fired from her teaching position at the university, and that brought even more financial uncertainty. Therefore, Ana took great notes, even to the point where she would write the jokes the teacher said in class, because she wanted to make sure she got everything that was important.

Ana completed university in 6 years instead of 7 and worked as well to help support her family. She then studied in Brazil and then in the United States. Ana is now a pediatrician in the United States, in the Bronx, and has her own pediatric clinic, helping those children who are most in need. Ana is a Latina female of strength and has demonstrated that no matter who you are or where you come from, you can accomplish anything you set your mind to. Ana was faced with much adversity and could have easily made excuses and not taken responsibility to find her way, but she didn't. She assumed the strength and the responsibility shown to her by her mother and her uncles.

9

Empathy and Tolerance

"Never look down on anybody unless you're helping them up."
- Jesse Jackson

In today's world it is important for us to remember and realize that as babies we are born without prejudice or bias. As babies, we are at our purest form, but then people, society and family beliefs mold us and tell us what is and what isn't. As a baby, we don't see color, we don't see race, we don't see gender or sexual preference. We are told by someone close to us, like parents, teachers, guardians, or government officials, their personal beliefs or perspectives based on how they were raised or what society has told them thus far, and often, we grow up having acquired the same thoughts and ideals which create who we are and what we project onto the world around us.

I am going to use a very simple example to demonstrate. You can probably pinpoint something that you do that others perceive as "different," or that others do that you perceive as "different." My examples include bread and coffee.

Does anyone keep their bread in the refrigerator? The first time I met someone that did, I thought it was the craziest thing in the world. Why would you need to keep bread in the refrigerator? Doesn't everyone know it goes in the cupboard?

Now how about coffee? Does anyone keep their coffee in the freezer? Well, I do! Yes, that's right, I keep my coffee in the freezer. Why? My very simple and logical response is that my Aunt Carmela always kept her coffee in the freezer, so I always thought that it was the best way to do it because she was the best cook in the world to me; she was a role model, so everything she does must be right. Right?

Can you see where I'm going with this? Our perceptions and pre-conditioned thoughts are why you and I think the way that we do today. What we have learned to do in our environment, is how we act today. While putting bread in the refrigerator and coffee in the freezer are harmless acts based on what we have been taught, we now need to look at more detrimental influences that we are taught growing up that cause hate, prejudice, low self-esteem, and bullying.

Empathy is the ability to understand and share the feelings of another person. A lot of trouble in today's world or even in your day-to-day life is due to a lack of understanding, communication, or misperception of information. How many times have you looked at or read an email, text message or social media post thinking it was rude or had some underlying meaning that wasn't really there at all? How could it? You can't hear the person's voice as you read it.

How about when you think someone looks at you a certain way or you think someone doesn't like you and you really have no basis for it other than what you think or what someone else has told you? Now on a much harsher level, what if a person calls you a derogatory name to try and hurt you or bully you through prejudice or racism, using words like Dike, Fag, Nigger, Half-Breed, Slant Eyes, Spic, Pig, Greaseball, etc. When you hear these words out of someone's mouth, you most likely react and want to pounce on them for their ignorance. No one usually stops and asks someone that says those things, "Why would you say that? Who taught you that? Why do you think that's ok to say?"

We are a reactive not a proactive society, but if we think about it, half of the discord and animosity towards each other today can be solved by better communication, more tolerance and understanding, and by asking more questions. Wouldn't you agree?

We are a multicultural society, and if we want to eventually have a world free of racism, prejudice, and limiting beliefs, then we need to practice being more openminded and show more kindness, compassion, and empathy. We need to understand that we are all different, and we need to be appreciated and valued for our individualism; that no single race, culture, or religion is better than another. We are all human beings, and we must love one another no matter who they are or where they come from. Right or wrong, we do what we do because it was instilled in us long before we realized there was another way of thinking or doing things, and the only way to change it is through education and helping others understand why people think the way they do.

Now let's look at some historical figures who we can learn more about, from different cultures, who practiced such understanding and tolerance and were able to move mountains and change the world through peace, nonviolence, love, tolerance and understanding. There are many, but the ones that come to my immediate mind are John Lewis, Jesus, Mother Teresa, as well as others I had mentioned before like Martin Luther King, Jr., Nelson Mandela, and Mahatma Gandhi. Read a book on each on these people, and you will see that they changed the world without lifting a finger or showing hate or violence towards anyone. Anyone can be seen and heard without showing hate or needing to be violent.

It is important sometimes to "agree to disagree." We won't always see eye-to-eye; however, we can learn to appreciate each other's opinions and perspectives, as well as realize that some people just aren't going to change. Therefore, what is my point?

My point is that if we want to change prejudice, and we want to change the way we think as a whole, to be kinder and more accepting, it needs to start with you. We need to be more proactive than reactive when looking to the future. Learning about different cultures and different ways of life are very important. The more we learn, the more understanding and forgiving we can be. We need to be tolerant, loving and forgiving.

What was instilled in your parents or grandparents gets instilled in you. Whether it be a stereotype, whether it be hatred for another person or group of people, whether it be a simple way of doing something or a limiting belief. We need not judge each other but understand their perspective and ask why they think this way, or why they do what they do. Then if detrimental, we must try to change that bias or belief, so it is not passed down to another generation.

Show compassion. We are all products of our environment, and therefore, the only way to change what we have been taught is to show people a kinder, better way. A great lesson from former Harlem Globetrotter, Herb Lang, "We need to understand where these thoughts came from, and once we try to understand them, we can start to form a conversation and build new relationships. We are all in this together. Children only know what they are taught. Let's reflect on those biases; let's reflect on what we are telling our children; let's take a deeper look into what we believe about the world and our society."

<u>The Story of Ria Story</u>
<u>Understanding Each Other's Journey</u>

"What happens to us influences us, there is no doubt… But HOW it influences us is what's most important. If your past is holding you back from reaching your potential, it's not serving you. Choose to let it go and move forward. You can't move forward very well if you are dragging the past behind you." - Ria Story

Ria Story is a motivational speaker and author, who shares her story with other people to help them get through traumatic experiences they have been faced with in their life. She is an amazing woman who has overcome incredible trauma herself to be where she is today. She grew up on a farm with her parents and brother, seeming fairly normal from the outside looking in. Ria was homeschooled, which made it easier to hide what was really happening behind closed doors. Ria was sexually abused by her father from the age of 12 to the age of 19 and even trafficked by him.

Ria's father started sexually abusing her when she was only 12 years old. It started out as how daddies and daughters should be close to one another; how God had given her to him to protect, so he could be sure that she was safe and taken care of. From there it really progressed. He took her clothes off; he told her the whole time what a perfect daughter she was, and God had given her to him as an answer to his problem.

Religion was used as a way to control Ria. Her dad would often say God gave her to him as an answer to being unfaithful to her mother. God had nothing to do with it; it was her father's way of manipulating her. This progressed as she got older, and by the age of 17, he was regularly having sex with her. He would also manipulate her for favors in exchange for something she wanted, like nights out with her friends. He would tie her up and beat her, take nude photos of her, and as she got older, he trafficked her to men that he would meet on the internet.

The situation got deeper and darker. It got to the point that she thought about taking her life. She could never see that there would be a way out. She was very isolated and controlled, and every time she tried to leave, her dad would go find her and bring her back.

Ria knew deep down that what was happening to her was wrong, that it shouldn't be happening. She often gets asked, "why didn't you leave," but there is so much emotional manipulation that it is difficult for anyone to understand if they haven't gone through it. He manipulated her by telling her that if she turned him in, he would go to hell and that no one would understand what they had.

She became a victim of her circumstances. She lacked self-confidence and was unable to help herself or anyone else. She didn't understand why this was happening to her. She says, "When you go through something like this, there is no sense of self-worth or self-love." She felt shame, which is different from guilt. To Ria guilt would mean she made a mistake, however, shame is that she was the mistake. She felt there was something wrong with her for this terrible situation to happen to her. It took a huge mindset shift for her to believe it was not her, and the caring of one person to get her out of the trauma she was living in.

At 19, Ria finally found someone who really and truly cared about her for who she was, and this is the point where Ria was able to break free from the abuse she was living. If it weren't for meeting her husband, she can never be sure what would have happened, as he was the first person she ever told. It wasn't until three months into their relationship that he knew something was wrong, and although everyone was telling him not to get involved, he cared too much to let her go. After reading all the signs, he finally asked her what was happening, and she told him. Finally, she was able to escape with his help.

At this point when Ria left home, she never wanted to look back. Her decision was to lock it up and just move forward. She didn't want to talk about it, not even with her husband. Eventually though, she was able to break the silence, and in 2013, after listening to a talk by motivational speaker Les Brown, she knew she had to tell her story to help herself and to help others. She found her "why" and finally realized that God does not cause the pain in our lives, but we can use it to give other people courage when we share our story. She realized she could help others and that everyone has pain, but it is what you do with it that matters most.

Her advice to those going through adversity or trauma, is don't be the victim. Find the strength inside to help yourself and get help from others. Then share your story and help someone else overcome what they are going through. Use the strength of your words and what has happened to you to inspire others to do the same and overcome what they are going thorough. What happens to us, influences us, but it doesn't determine or define who we become. You don't have to make bad choices or feel unworthy for the rest of your life because of something you experienced. Her final thought, "if I can give just one person hope, it makes it all worth it."

10

Success: What is it?

"The way to get started is to quit talking and begin doing."
- Walt Disney

People get a little bit confused about success. What does success mean to you? What does it look like to be a successful person? The definition of success is different for everyone. Some define it as the dollar amount in their bank account. Others define it based on happiness. Others think it is being able to do what you want when you want. I feel successful when I know I am working on something that excites me and doesn't make me want to hit the snooze button when my alarm goes off in the morning.

If success were measured as the dollar amount in one's bank account, then I would have to say I am a very unsuccessful person at this moment, but I do not believe in that definition of success, because there are moments in this life that we have ups and downs, but we still remain successful within ourselves. We cannot discredit the work we have done in the past; we cannot discredit our attitude and love for life, because there are pit stops along the way, but that does not mean that we are not successful as people or as human beings.

There are many things to celebrate in one's life as being a success, waking up this morning was a success; graduation is a success; making the team is a success; and so on. Sometimes we need to be careful how we define success. While it's great to achieve that end goal of having wealth and things we want to have, we need to take the journey to get to that point. As young people you often want instant or overnight success, but unfortunately, ninety-nine percent of the time it doesn't work that way. The journey is just as important as the success.

We are constantly bombarded by images of wealth on social media. We are inundated with people trying to sell get rich quick schemes, however, most of them are just that, schemes. They don't work, and if by the rare chance they do work, they don't last, and the reason they don't last is because many haven't been taught what to do with the money to keep it once they have it.

Let's go back to the person who defines success as having a lot of money. We must remember that most people who have a lot of money today also started with nothing. Take a moment to think of someone that you admire or wish you could have their success. Now go and find their story. I can almost guarantee they started with struggles and adversity, and some even lost it all and got it back again.

We need to make sure that when we hear people talk, that we don't get discouraged about our personal situation at the moment, because everybody, unless they were born into great wealth, had to get there somehow. It all started from nothing, and I think first it's more important to be successful within, or else you won't achieve that final goal for yourself, whatever it may be.

So, we need to be careful when we listen to outside influences that give their definition of success. I feel I'm a very successful person. However, depending on how you personally define the word some would probably think that at this moment I am far from the vision of success because I have just experienced losing most of what I worked for in the past five years, but I take responsibility for that, and I don't make excuses. Now, if I were to give up and stop here, then I would agree, I would not be successful.

Sometimes we need to look at these things as having happened for a reason. We need to change our perspective.

Many times, a door closes so that another one opens, and we can move to our greater potential. So, for me success is waking up every morning and knowing that I am doing exactly what I love to do, knowing that I have a plan, I have goals, I have a vision, I have dreams that aren't just in my mind but that I'm taking action towards achieving them.

Sometimes the idea of success gets distorted. So, when I think of the most successful people in the world I think of immigrants. I want you to picture them leaving their home country to come to America for a better life. I want you to think about the families that first came; young boys who came over by themselves, my great-grandmother came to the United States with her 5 sisters, and she was the youngest. She was 7 and her oldest sister was 21 but none of them spoke English. They were all girls; they were alone, and their parents were already in America. Why did people take this big leap into the unknown? Because America was said to be the land of opportunity, and where they were from, what they had, was nothing, often there wasn't even food to eat.

So, many people chose to make a better life for themselves and for their family, and they went into the unknown to try and create something better. Could you imagine being on that boat and you're almost to New York, and you look up to see the Statue of Liberty? You're about to get off this big boat with all of these people, with all of these different languages around you, and you walk into this room filled with hundreds of people, of different nationalities. The one side of you is probably scared and the other side of you, is filled with excitement.

At this moment, these people were successful, because they took action on their dream, followed through and made it to America. They didn't have any money in their bank account. They didn't have any idea as to what awaited them on the other side of the door, but they were successful in accomplishing that goal. Life is a series of goals and accomplishments, each one leading to something bigger and the ultimate dream or vision you have for yourself. In order for anybody to be successful, you really need to work towards achieving it. These people by just reaching Ellis Island were successful. They had no money; they were still on their journey, but they made it this far in accomplishing their dream.

The Story of Paul Kazanofski
An Immigrant's Road To Success

"I get more fulfillment from watching other people succeed, because I have everything I ever wanted, and I want others to be able to do the same."
– Paul Kazanofski

At the age of 4, Paul Kazanofski escaped communist Macedonia through Greece with his family and immigrated to Canada. His life did not look anything like it does today, as he is at the top of his business in real estate. His parents divorced a year after arriving in Canada, and he grew up without his father until they reunited 15 years later. Growing up in Point St. Charles, in Montreal, Quebec, his mom raised him in poverty, with a scarcity mindset and little hope of ever changing his circumstances.

As with many immigrants, fitting into a new culture brings other challenges as well. Coming from Macedonia, he needed to learn French and English. As a result of being dyslexic, he struggled through school. The streets were lined with delinquency, drugs, and crime. However, his mom was very strict and got him involved in whatever activities she could to keep him off the streets.

His early life was that of survival. Being bullied as a young boy, at the age of 8, his mom took matters into her own hands and brought him to the local gym, to meet a trainer to teach him how to box. This was where he found his passion, and his focus went into boxing. Boxing gave him the hope of becoming something other than nothing, and he aspired to one day be a professional boxer.

So, how did he become the millionaire entrepreneur that he is today? As soon as he knew he could leave home and go off on his own, he did. When he was 19, he went to California to meet his aunt and uncle on his father's side of the family. They were in real estate, and for the first time in his life, he saw how wealthy people lived, which was beyond his wildest dreams. He sold what little he had and illegally immigrated to the United States.

His necessity to survive taught him how to make money anywhere at any time. Buying anything he could for as little as he could, he would fix it up and sell it to someone else for double. It was in audio sales, selling speakers and surround sound systems, where he got his big break to start making significant amounts of money. His ability to master the art of negotiation and the art of the pitch were an important component to how he made his fortune.

Eventually, Paulie bought out the owner of the company, and while the other salesmen were going out drinking and to clubs, he saved everything he earned because he had one focus; he still had in his mind that he would become a world champion boxer. The discipline he got from boxing ultimately showed up in every area of his life to accomplish his goals.

When the business started taking off, he began to learn everything he could about sales and being an entrepreneur. He listened to tapes by Earl Nightingale and Jim Rohn, who taught him how to properly speak to and do business with other people. His motivation and determination to prosper got him to where he is today.

Now fast forward to when he started making incredible amounts of money, Paulie had one very serious problem. He was an illegal immigrant in the United States and could not open a bank account to keep his money in the bank. Therefore, his storage place of choice was his freezer! He wrapped his money in foil to make it look like meat in case anyone tried to rob him. After storing it there over an extended period of time, he decided to one day count the money he had in the freezer.

After thawing it out, to his surprise, he had about a million dollars! He was only 22 years old.

Not knowing what to do, he bought a house in Las Vegas in his girlfriend's name, which is how he stumbled into real estate. He then built a custom home and paid everything in cash. Thinking he would live there, he and his girlfriend were ready to move in, and someone came and wanted to buy the house for way more than he put into it. This gave him the idea to start building custom homes with a contractor. At this time, he was still boxing; he still had the speaker business and now he was into building and selling houses. When the market crashed in 2008, it was no longer lucrative to build houses, so he started buying and flipping properties.

Paul Kazanofski's story is one of true entrepreneurial success. The lesson is that no matter who you are or where you come from you can have it all, if you are disciplined, focused, motivated, and determined to do it. Today, he loves to show others how to do the same, and he spends a lot of time coaching and mentoring people to do as he did. He states, "I get more fulfillment from watching other people succeed, because I have everything I ever wanted, and I want others to be able to do the same." A true inspiration.

11

<u>Thoughts: What Do I Want?</u>

"The future belongs to those who believe in the beauty of their dreams."
– Eleanor Roosevelt

All of our goals and dreams begin with a thought, and so in this chapter, we will talk about the power of your mind, as your mind ultimately helps you believe or not believe the things that you can do in this life. So, I wanted to take a closer look into your thoughts because your thoughts ultimately power what you do or don't do in life.

We are bombarded by thousands of thoughts every day, and your dominant thoughts are what create your reality. If you are often having thoughts of doubt and negativity, then most likely you are not being very successful in your daily activities. However, if your thoughts are more on the optimistic side, then you likely see things as happening for a reason, and usually that reason is to your benefit.

Do you have a morning routine, or do you just roll out of bed and scramble to get ready for the day? I always start my day with a prayer on an app that I read, and it gets me in the right mindset for the day. I sit quietly for five minutes after that to reflect on what I read and listen to the silence because oftentimes the best things come to our minds when we just allow ourselves to sit in silence and quiet everything else around us. I then state 10 things I am grateful for as I had mentioned in the chapter on gratitude.

Our thoughts and goals should be written down. I have a vision board that I use for long-term goals, and I use an agenda for daily and weekly goals. I look at my vision board every day to remind myself of what I want to accomplish and what it will look like. This helps me keep those goals in my mind, and it helps me to focus on doing things each day that are small steps to get to those things I want in my life. One further step other than seeing them, I also make statements as if I already have what it is that I am working towards. This helps me believe that I can get to that point in my life. So, as I write this book, every day I say, "I am so grateful that I finally wrote my first book, and it has been a great success!" This just reaffirms that I am going to do it, and it will happen.

The biggest reason why people often fail to do what they set out for themselves is because their thoughts are not aligned with what they want. We often create an inner monologue telling ourselves what we can or cannot do; what we think we do or do not deserve. Depending on what you are thinking will ultimately depend on how your day or your accomplishments will go. If you've tried to do something before and it has "failed," it is probably because inside of you, you were telling yourself that you can't do it, or you didn't put a lot of effort into it, and therefore, stopped trying. Remember we are part of a culture at this moment that likes instant gratification and likes things to happen quickly; social media is proof of this. Therefore, it is important to learn patience when working to achieve your goals, as most things take time.

We need to really pay attention to what we're telling ourselves. If you are on social media every day filling your head with negativity and, for lack of better terms, garbage, then your mind is going to be consumed with those thoughts. I often tell my students who are struggling with depression, anxiety, low self-esteem, family pressures or anything else, to create at least five positive "I am" statements. I then have them put the statements on the wall or in their bathroom next to their mirror, wherever it might be, and they look themselves in the mirror and say those statements at the beginning and end of each day. Some examples could be I am unique, I am strong, I am beautiful, I am honest, I am successful, I am the best and only me, and so on. By doing these things first thing in the morning you create an energy that is much healthier for you to carry out your day.

Another common reason people tend to fall short of their goals is because they have an all or nothing approach. They see the big picture, the end goal, which is great, but they didn't plan the steps to get there, and so they say tomorrow I am going to start, and then they don't have time to do it, so they say, "oh I'm never going to do it!"

The reality is that things come up, and you need to be forgiving of yourself. A habit usually requires about 90 days of doing something the same way repetitively before it becomes a habit. Meaning it will take time to change and do something to make it habitual. You can go to a weekend workshop with the idea that you will change your life, and that is great for a jumpstart. Three days can put you in a good mindset, but three days is not going to change your overall habits that you already have unless you are consistent.

So, when you set out to make a change, do something new, or begin a new goal, you need to start small. Take those small steps. Remember, the Great Wall of China is massive when you look at the whole thing; it is amazing. However, in order to become that grand wall, it needed to start with laying each individual brick one-by-one. Now think of the wall as your goal and think of the bricks as the steps that you need to take in order to create your goal. All goals start with a single thought, and when you take action, those thoughts can become reality.

The Story of Maria Trusa
The Power of the Mind

"There is no human being alive who doesn't have a gift or a talent, something good to share with this world. Focusing on that is the cornerstone of empowerment and success. There are no limits to the heights we can reach when our self-esteem is reinforced." – Maria Trusa

Maria Trusa is a native of the Dominican Republic, from a small town called Licey al Medio, near Santiago and Moca. She was one of five children, and this is where she spent the early years of her life. She lived with her mom and dad. She knew her father as a good man for a few years but unfortunately, he became an alcoholic, and this destroyed her family. Her mother got to a point where she couldn't take it anymore. Maria and her siblings were living in multiple different houses as a child because her father didn't pay the rent, and they were thrown out of the house. She remembers always walking around without shoes, which she got used to and her mother took used clothes from other people and sewed them into clothing Maria could wear.

Maria remembers that her mother always kept her and the home clean and organized even though they were poor, but a point came when her mom needed to do something because she had no money or food to care for Maria and her siblings. This is when the more difficult times began. Her mother had an opportunity to go to the United States with her two oldest brothers, where she felt they could at least work and send money back to the children to eat and live. At eight years old she was left to care for herself and live with another family. However, the tragedy that would leave the mark she would carry with her for the rest of her life, and almost kill her, came at the age of nine.

One night can ruin your entire life, and at the age of nine Maria's father, the man that was supposed to protect her, gave her to a strange man to resolve a debt, and this man brutally raped her, but he didn't just rape her. He forced her to drink an entire bottle of whisky without stopping, and this bottle of whisky could have killed her. She thanks God that she had that bottle of whisky because it is probably what saved her life, as it allowed her to not feel the pain of the man that was repeatedly hurting her over and over again.

After this one night that scarred the rest of her life, Maria went into a deep depression. She cried every day, and she wanted to die. However, after her mom had returned to care for her and time had gone by Maria still had no desire to live, until one day her mother yelled at her and told her she needed to live, she needed to get up; she needed to be strong because life was going to continue. Although in this moment, Maria was shocked at her mother and resented her many years for being so cold hearted, she later thanked her, because had her mother not done this, she may never have come out of her depression. After it happened, it was never spoken about again until many years later.

At the age of 15, Maria went to the United States, and she remembers walking out of the airport and knowing in her mind that God had something better for her, and she put it in her mind, perhaps without realizing, that she was meant for greatness. It was not easy; there were challenges everywhere she turned. School was difficult. She went from being a great student in the Dominican Republic to not doing well because she didn't speak the language, and at that time, there weren't any bilingual programs. She passed her days in school understanding nothing and failing.

After 6 months of arriving, things started to click, and she was able to begin to understand. She eventually graduated from high school, and after overcoming the language barrier in high school, she was then faced with rejection time and again in finding a job because of her accent. Bound and determined this wouldn't hold her back, she took classes to help with her accent. As well, Maria was faced with the challenges of being married at 17 and being a young mother, all while still working to accomplish her dreams. The one thing for everyone to realize is that despite all the challenges and all the continued struggles, she has created an incredible life for herself and for her children.

Maria is now the CEO of Formé, a medical clinic in White Plains, New York, and with her autobiographical book, she is the founder of the movement #YoDigoNoMas… I Say No More. For Maria, she will do whatever it takes to bring awareness to break the silence of women, children and men who are going through or have gone through similar abuse to show them they can still create the life of their dreams as she did.

12

Desire: How bad do you want it?

"The starting point of all achievement is desire."
– Napoleon Hill

Napoleon Hill is the author of the book "Think and Grow Rich." He went out and interviewed the world's top achievers in the early 1900's and published his findings in 1937. The first step of the thirteen towards riches is desire. The one thing he found among the world's top achievers was that above all else their desire to accomplish their goals was unwavering. He also stated that this is why the majority of people quit and don't accomplish their dreams, simply because the desire to succeed is not greater than the effort needed to achieve them.

If you have set goals for yourself or have ever created a vision board, you will need to ask yourself why. You should reflect on goals that you have set and accomplished successfully and ones that you have given up on. Most likely, those that you accomplished had attached to them a strong desire to do so, and those that you didn't accomplish probably didn't have a real reason or purpose attached to them to make you want to be successful in striving to achieve them.

You need to ask yourself why you want something because it is ultimately going to be the driving force behind your success. If you want something simply because everyone else is doing it or because it is what someone else wants you to do, then most likely you will not be successful in accomplishing that task, unless you are a people pleaser and allow that to drive you. However, if you are connected to your purpose and understand why you have set a specific goal for yourself, then you will most likely succeed.

Another reason people don't accomplish what they set out to do is simply because they don't believe they can do it, or something else is much stronger in their mind which ultimately sabotages them. Here's an example:

Let's look at getting good grades. Most likely, you and most people you know can do well in school. However, whether or not it is important to you is completely different. There might be something else you prefer doing, and therefore the desire to do that something else outweighs your desire to study and do better in school. People often set a goal for themselves, but they find little success in achieving it if their desire to do it does not outweigh everything else.

How many times have you made a New Year's resolution only to find that by February, you did not stick to it? Why is that? It's probably because the idea to do it might be there, we might really like the idea of our goal, but the desire to achieve it isn't there. We have to ask ourselves why do we want it? Do we want it because we want to be healthier? Do we want it because society says I should have it? Do we want it because we deserve it? Do we want it because we know we won't achieve it? Yes, that's right, we do set goals for ourselves to self-sabotage. So, these are the important questions to ask when setting a goal for yourself because they will ultimately determine whether you will succeed.

Therefore, when you're working to accomplish a goal, you really need to ask why this, and how important is it to me. These two questions will determine your desire to follow through and accomplish it.

The Story of Jonte Hall
If You Really Want It, You Can Have It

"We all go through pitstops. Don't let it define who you are as a person. Don't give up on your dreams no matter what. As long as your heart stands tall, you're not so small." – Jonte Hall

Jonte Hall is a former Harlem Globetrotter, and his story is one that shows both desire and perseverance. What he wanted was to become a professional basketball player, but no one, and I mean no one ever believed he would. Why, might you ask? Because at his tallest, he is 5 feet 2 inches.

Jonte grew up in inner-city Baltimore, and from a young age he loved basketball. He was surrounded by a great many things that a lot of people don't experience every day, like drugs, gangs, and violence, but he did not waiver on his love for the game. At the age of six he received his first basketball, and he "fell in love." As he grew up, his friends began to respect that he was into basketball and that was his focus, even though many of them were not going in the right direction. As well, his mother would always walk him to school, and while it may have been embarrassing at the time, he is grateful, because it kept him away from the trouble that he could have encountered had she not been there.

The difficulty for Jonte was that as he got older, he did not grow, but he knew he had the skill. One can imagine that when you are not even five feet tall in high school, you are not taken seriously when telling people, you are going to be a great basketball player. He was faced daily with naysayers and people who attempted to stomp on his dreams.

In his senior year, his aunt helped him write letters to different colleges and universities to have them come and watch him play. He thought if they could just see what he could do on the basketball court, they would think differently about his height and see his ability to be a serious athlete. However, no offers came, and he walked on to the team at the community college he attended after high school.

While he did not get the big break he was hoping for, Jonte still remained hopeful and still believed his day would come, but he could not prepare for what would happen next. His mother was diagnosed with MS (Multiple Sclerosis), a disease of the central nervous system, and he had to leave college to go to work to help his mom. This was a difficult moment for him.

For Jonte, this was a pitstop, and he says you can't get stuck at the pitstops as they are a part of life. He said everything he did, even as a janitor cleaning bathrooms, he did with pride and to the best of his ability, because he knew that would not be his final destination. Many years later, at the age of 25, he went to his mom and said he still wanted to play basketball. He still knew in his heart he could do this. His mother gave him her blessing, and he started going to tryouts for different minor league teams.

This was not an easy task for Jonte, because he was rejected over and over again, and as one can imagine his height played a huge role. However, he kept hopeful because he was never told that his talent wasn't there, and just as he was about to give up, he gave it one more shot. Jonte emailed the Washington Generals, who were the Harlem Globetrotters' opponents, and finally all his perseverance and efforts of never giving up paid off.

The Washington Generals gave him a contract, which wasn't much financially, however, it meant everything to be playing basketball and getting paid for it. He stayed with them for a year and a half, and the Globetrotters loved him so much, that they gave him a tryout and was contracted by them.

Throughout Jonte's whole career he was told he wouldn't make it, and now he is in the history books as the shortest Harlem Globetrotter ever. His advice for young people today, "Just hang in there, go through your pitstops. You might have jobs you don't want to be at, but they are not meant for you to stay there. Don't give up on your dreams. You will always be tested by God, but have faith because if you do, He will get you to where you are supposed to be. We all go through pitstops. Don't let it define who you are as a person. Don't give up on your dreams no matter what. As long as your heart stands tall, you're not so small."

13

Faith

"Faith is taking the first step even when you don't see the whole staircase." – Martin Luther King Jr.

Faith is defined as complete trust or confidence in someone or something. It is your ability to believe no matter what that you will accomplish the desires that you have and the goals that you set for yourself. A lot of times we hear this word in religion. For example, walk by faith and not by sight, and this is a very interesting phrase because to walk by faith means that you are doing things everyday knowing the outcome will be in your favor.

A lot of times it is used in religion for God. We cannot see God, yet many people believe and have faith that there is a God and that he does exist in some other form that we cannot see. The idea of faith, or that something will happen that has not yet already happened, instills in us as well a sense of hope.

Let me give you an example, if I were to have a crystal ball and could tell you that all your dreams will come true, do you really need to have faith today in order to make that happen? The answer is no. If we knew the outcome of our life and what will happen the next day and the next day and the next, there would be no need for faith because we would know what would be. So, walking by faith is knowing those things will happen, you will accomplish your goals and not need to worry along the way.

Having faith is literally saying to yourself that those things that you want in your life are going to happen and believing that they will. Having faith is knowing that God, or if you don't believe in God, then the universe, exists in one form or another to create the things that you want in this lifetime. Those people who continuously achieve their goals, achieve their dreams, one-by-one achieved them through faith. I am going to share with you the idea of unwavering faith and the fact that you know that whatever it is that you want can happen, can be achieved, if you have the faith within to believe it.

Remember that life is like driving on a dark road. You can only see as far in front of you as the headlights, however, you know the road is there and will take you to your final destination. This is faith. You have the thought, the idea, and you move forward. You can only see one step at a time; however, you know that each step will bring you closer to your goal. When you know this deep within, you will never feel worry or anxiety again.

Remember, if you knew what your future held, and that in a certain period of time your dreams would come true or you would attain your goals, you would wake up every morning excited and happy because you would know it was going to happen. The lesson to be learned here is that you have the control to believe the same. You can wake up every morning and tell yourself that you are one day closer to achieving exactly what you want because you control your thoughts and your mind.

I can't even contain myself every time I go over this, and you may wonder why I am so sure. It is because it has personally happened to me. In 2014, I created a vision board, and, on that vision board was a school, certain clothing items from a store that I love, a beautiful home with a pool, a red convertible car and a mystery man face with a question mark on it. I believed I would have it all. I woke up every morning knowing it was coming. In 2016, I started my own school. I got a red car which was great even if it wasn't a convertible. After that I was making enough money to buy these certain clothes from the store that I really liked, and a year after that I was renting a beautiful house with a pool. Everything came except the mystery man, but I didn't put a lot of concentration on him, eventually that will come. So, you see, faith works, things happen, and if you are still doubting, I have other examples as well, but for now, try it. You will see.

The Story of Roberto Mendoza
Seeing Is Not Believing, Believing Is Seeing

"If you believe, nothing is impossible." – Roberto Mendoza

An image of Roberto Mendoza should be placed in the dictionary next to the word *faith*. He is the vision of strength and truth that no matter who you are or where you come from you can truly achieve anything you want. He is a world-renowned executive chef for celebrities, presidents, and royalty, but looking at who he is today, you would never imagine what he had to overcome. The one thing that he always had with him no matter the circumstance was his faith.

Roberto was born in El Salvador. He lived with his grandmother because his parents abandoned him at a young age. He grew up in a warzone and in extreme poverty; he had little clothing and barely enough food to eat, often going to bed hungry. His faith was the only thing that got him through everything and gave him hope for the future.

When he was studying at university, the country was in a civil war, and being a student put him in danger. He couldn't use a backpack because the military would think he was carrying weapons, and he had to carry all of his materials in his arms back and forth to school every day. One day on his way to school, he was captured by the military and held for many days.

After he was released and set free, he was accepted as a refugee and permitted entry into Canada. It was difficult for him to acclimate to the climate, live alone and learn a whole new language, which was French. He did it and was grateful for the opportunity to be free from his war-torn country, but he wanted better for himself and especially warmer weather.

Roberto moved to Los Angeles where he had some family and was able to live with his aunt for a short time. He tried to find a job, as he had studied accounting in university, but he couldn't find work because he didn't speak English. He wanted to do well and help others, but his aunt wanted him to be realistic, get a job to support himself and then if there was anything left, he could think of others. Although he was surrounded by people who tried to destroy his dreams, he continued to fight and believe he could have the life he deserved.

Eventually Roberto had to take any job he could to support himself, and he began washing dishes in a restaurant run by a Jewish family. Here is where he began learning to prep food, and little by little, he went from cutting to cooking. As well he learned to speak Hebrew and of course English. Roberto loved his job and felt as though all would be well finally, but soon he was met with an unexpected reality. His aunt and uncle made him leave their home, and he had nowhere to go.

At this time, Roberto didn't have enough money to rent an apartment, so he lived in his car. When Roberto wasn't working, all he did was read the Bible and pray, knowing that his faith would present to him another opportunity. That opportunity soon came in the form of a challenge when a very important customer came to the restaurant and wanted the head chef's salmon dish. However, the head chef was not there on this day, and they didn't know what to do. Roberto recognized this as the opportunity he was waiting for and took it. The client turned out to be the Prince of Saudi Arabia, and Roberto's salmon dish turned out to be extraordinary. The prince liked it so much that he only wanted Roberto to cook for him in the future. This was the beginning of Roberto's fame as a chef.

Roberto was so proud of what he was able to accomplish, and in the next few years, he only had time for work. One would think that all was perfect for Roberto, but he was soon confronted with another tremendous setback. Roberto was deported from the United States and told that his documents were not real. He was held for a while and then discovered that the notary who filed his paperwork didn't do it correctly, and he was put in jail. At this moment he actually thought about taking his life because he couldn't imagine going back to El Salvador.

Roberto did not take his life and was sent back to El Salvador only to have to start over again in his country. With little hope of being able to return to the United States, his grandmother reminded him that with God anything is possible. Roberto did not quit fighting and would not be defeated, so he decided to open his own restaurant in San Salvador. However, as soon as he opened his new restaurant, an Earthquake came and destroyed everything he just built. Once again, he lost everything. He couldn't believe this was happening.

After this disaster, Roberto took it as a sign that God had a different plan for him, and the next day he went to the American Embassy to request another Visa, believing that miracles could happen, and they did. Roberto was able to get another Visa which was virtually impossible, and he returned to the United States.

Over the years, Roberto has done what he calls, "the work of God," believing he was brought back to the United States to work for A-list celebrities, so that he could continue his mission to help those in need. Today, Roberto travels the world helping the underserved communities by providing them with food, and caring for as many children as he can, so they don't have to go hungry like he did when he was a child.

For Roberto, education is necessary to stop poverty, but more importantly faith is necessary to help you continue believing there is a way when you don't see a way. Roberto has always asked God for whatever he needed and wrote it down. One thing he wrote was, "Help me help others." Eventually, Roberto won $250,000 dollars on a lottery ticket, and with that money, he began his foundation. He says, "If you believe, nothing is impossible." In his community, Roberto is the hope for the hopeless. He feeds thousands of people every week, and he truly lives his life to serve.

14

<u>Action</u>
<u>What Steps Will You Take to Create Your Success?</u>

Action is the foundational key to all success. – Pablo Picasso

A thought is only a thought, and a dream is only a dream until you take action towards doing something about it. Writing your goals and creating a vision board are action steps, as they give you the right mindset and make you remember what you are working to achieve. Now, to make them happen, you need to take action. You can visualize and believe it will happen, but without taking action everything remains a thought and a vision. The reality is that there is very little chance someone would come to the door and randomly give you exactly what you want, right? So, taking action means doing things that will bring you closer to your dreams and goals.

Let's think of a modern-day example. Let's say you really want to start a podcast, and you want to interview people to have them tell their stories to then create a book to inspire people to believe they can achieve success no matter who they are or where they come from. However, you don't have many followers on social media, and nobody really knows who you are. You have this great idea, you want to inspire others, but you don't know where to start; you don't feel people will listen or you won't get great interview guests. Well, you are starting out by fueling your mind with negativity.

Here is the key… just do it! If you just sit there and do nothing, then you certainly won't have any chance at creating what you want. It doesn't matter how many followers you have or whether you are well known in the world. What matters is what you want to say and why you want to say it. So, first take those thoughts and visions and ask yourself, "what can I do

119

today to make them a reality?" You are not going to have a number one podcast or a bestselling book overnight. If you are merely looking to become famous without a reason for it, you will most likely give up because the road to success is not an easy one, and without a mission and purpose that is bigger than you are, it will be a great challenge.

Next, write a letter and send it to people that you would be interested in interviewing. Make sure they align with your purpose and just send it. At this moment, I just broke 900 followers on Instagram, not many, however two months ago that was only about 450. It is not the number of followers you have; it is the quality of followers you have. I know people who have bought followers, and the problem with buying followers is simply that they don't really have an interest in what you are doing, you were just a pop-up add for them to follow, and they did. Remember quality, not quantity.

I have interviewed some great people. How did this happen? First and foremost because I took action and just asked. That's right! It was as simple as writing that DM or sending an email. Mind you I had multiple people that didn't respond, but I had multiple people that did and said YES! The second reason for getting great interviews was because people related to my mission, and the work I am doing. You are the gate keeper to bringing your thoughts and dreams to fruition. It's as simple as that.

So, in interviewing these people, what was it that they all had in common to achieving their goals and dreams? They all took action! As well, they added in some of the other pieces of the success equation that were written about like desire, thoughts, faith and perseverance. Just remember, you need not know exactly how you are going to reach your goals, however taking small deliberate action each day will get you to where you want to be.

The Story of Ram Castillo
Strategic Action Gets You Where You Want To Be

"Zoom out. Play the long game. Be patient. Enjoy the journey. Learn, gather, and mold yourself inside because these are what the greats of the world have in common. So go for what you really want. Say what you want. Believe you will get it and go for it. Don't dig up seeds right after you plant them. Nurture them and put in the work to allow them to grow."
— Ram Castillo

When you hear the story of Ram Castillo, you are going to be uplifted by what he has accomplished and the action steps he took to achieve his goals. However, you will also feel a deep ache in your heart for the young boy who had to endure so much to get there.

Ram Castillo was born in the Philippines and immigrated to Australia with his mom and dad when he was just a toddler. His dad was one of eleven children, and his mother was one of five. Growing up neither of his parents had much. They lived a life in the Philippines that was very underdeveloped when his parents were growing up. He would hear stories of his father growing up with a tablespoon of peanut butter and a piece of bread to share with the whole family, and that would be all they had to eat for the day.

His family's struggles are what difficult really looks like. If you're from a westernized world, you can work in McDonald's and still earn 3 or 4 times more than someone working an office job in the Philippines. Growing up for his parents was survival, so they used education to separate themselves and create opportunities. His dad had two bachelor's degrees, Marine Transportation and Mechanical Engineering. However, his mom had a different scenario growing up. Her father was a womanizer; he was violent, and her mother often supported them however she could.

When Ram migrated to Australia with his family, it was difficult to move from a country where you are surrounded by friends and family. Also, it was very disheartening for his dad. In the Philippines, his dad was a Mechanical Engineer, however when they got to Australia, their university degrees were not recognized, and his dad had no choice but to work in a factory. Raising three kids on a factory salary was difficult, but the one thing that Ram never saw was his dad complain.

This shaped Ram because his version of hard was different than what his parents went through. As a child, he often thought, *"why do other people have more stuff than I do,"* even though he didn't consider his family to be poor. They were just less well off. However, what they did have in abundance was a lot of love, a lot of community, a lot of sharing and a lot of laughter. The abundance of love from home was what would get him through the struggles to come in school.

As a child, Ram didn't have toys, so he would collect things around the house to play with and build whatever he could imagine. One day when he was four, his mom asked him what he wanted to be when he grows up, and he told her he didn't know; he said he just wanted to make stuff. In that moment, he clearly remembers her saying, "You can be whatever you want to be, just dream big," and this always stayed with him.

Ram was always allowed to dream, be curious and explore whatever he wanted. His parents were wonderful and allowed him to dream and believe he could be and do whatever he set his mind to. Although they may not have had a lot, Ram believes that this gift of allowing him to believe he can be anything was priceless.

Ram was a small boy without great luxuries as other children had, and because of this he was severely bullied. He had his arm broken 3 times and 16 stitches by the age of 11 due to bullying in school. The students were suspended and eventually expelled, but this small boy went to school every day in fear. School was not a safe place for him, but he found the courage to just kept going. In his mind, there was no alternative, and it was the love and support of his parents and friends that helped him through this terrible experience that no child should ever have to go through. He is just grateful that there was so much love at home. He believes it outweighed the trauma, and he was determined that it would not hold him back.

Another part that played an important role for Ram and his family was their faith. Faith that everything would be all right; faith that good would come from the struggles they faced, and this gave them peace in the difficult moments.

Ram is also an inspiration in the lesson of not letting his pride stop him from getting what he wanted. He went to a design school that wasn't one of the top schools in Australia because his family couldn't afford it, but he did get a scholarship to another design school, and he was talented. When he finished, he took a job in the mailroom at Ogilvy, a lead advertising company in Sydney and around the world. People around him thought he was crazy for just finishing design school and going to work in a mailroom when he had gone to school on scholarship for his talent. Ram didn't see it that way. He saw it as a great strategy to get close to the people he wanted to be around, and he was right.

In the first week of working his mailroom job, he had met multiple people who were working on some of the biggest accounts in the world. He didn't see it the way others did, and from early on he knew what it meant to pay your dues, work for it and not be given anything. Ram built his career from learning, starting at the bottom, and getting his foot in the door. He found fulfillment in learning, in climbing and in the journey.

Ram's advice for his high school self, if he were able to go back and give himself advice, "Trust in the process and really focus on mastery. So many people try things and then give up, but they haven't really given it enough time, so they ultimately give up before really working on it." Today so many people want instant gratification, and even for himself sometimes, but no one can truly be good at what they do without first putting in the work. We can all be gold medalists and record holders if we want to be, but it is not something that comes instantly. If you want to put in the time, sacrifice and challenges, then you can do it too. It all depends on how bad you want it.

"Remember, the people that we praise in public have spent years and years in private working on their craft to achieve what they have. Don't get lost in the "feed." It's a filtered feed. We see the finished product. A person's success is like an iceberg. What you see at the surface, for example the images on social media, is just a small part of what is actually there. Meaning what you see today from someone you admire is the product of many other things that you have not seen in order for them to achieve what they have today."

15

Perseverance and Resilience

"Every strike brings me closer to the next home run." – Babe Ruth

With the speed of internet, entertainment, and all the constant stimulation we are surrounded with every day, we tend to always want instant gratification, instant success, instant answers, and waiting has become a thing that quite honestly no one wants to wait for!

However, most things in life, especially our dreams, do not come about overnight, and usually take months if not years to create. This is why so many people do not follow their dreams and revert to old ways, old habits or old jobs. It's because they want immediate results, and immediate results in achieving the big goal don't usually happen. It is the little step taken each day that gets you to the big goal or dream. Ask anyone who has been successful in achieving their vision for their life and very few will say it took a week or a month.

This is where resilience comes in and what it means to be a resilient person. A lot of times in our life we have setbacks and a lot of times because of those setbacks we tend to talk to ourselves in a discouraging manner. For example, something that you had planned out in your mind doesn't necessarily go well and automatically after it doesn't go well you think, "well I can't do that, it's never going to happen. I'm no good at this." However, you only gave it one shot maybe two. Even Stephen King got rejected 30 times before someone finally published his first book! Imagine if he gave up after the first few tries.

Resilience is defined as the capacity to recover quickly from difficulties. It is the toughness within you to get back up and try again. Sometimes we set goals for ourselves that aren't realistic and sometimes we do this subconsciously to set ourselves up for failure. Now I know that sounds crazy, but we don't realize it when we do it, so understanding that you can set high goals and high expectations for yourself is great, however when you don't achieve that goal specifically, but you have shown improvement towards making that goal a reality, then you need to celebrate it.

Let me give you another example. Let's say you don't do well in Math. So, you get a failing grade, and you say to yourself, "Ok, I am going to get an A on the next test." You then study really hard, and the next time you go to take the test, you only get a C. Now, you didn't exactly achieve the goal that you set for yourself, but you were successful in doing better. Do you get down on yourself because you didn't accomplish what you set out to do, or do you applaud yourself because you did accomplish doing better? This is often where we subconsciously sabotage ourselves. We set a very high goal, and while it may be possible eventually, it will usually take more than one attempt in working to achieve it. So, you need to ask yourself, are you the person that would quit and say, "It's no use, I'm just not good at this, or would you say ok, I am getting closer, and I will keep working at it?"

Now on another aspect you say that you are going to start a new routine, and for a week you stick with it. Every morning you get up, write your goals, exercise, eat healthier, and then you have one bad day. Do you start again the next day, or do you give up? If you give up and ignore the seven good days, then you need to ask yourself why. It was one bad day, but you had seven really good days. You see we tend to focus on the negative in a situation and not look at the steps that we've taken that were positive or beneficial to us. So instead of saying to yourself, "I can't do this; I always fail eventually; this is impossible," you should be telling yourself, "I had seven really good days, and I had one set back. That's ok. I'm going to get back on track; I am going to continue doing what I had done for the past seven days."

You need to be able to be resilient, to come back quickly and not allow your mind to interrupt the habit that you had before. You can't stop and just give up on whatever the goal is that you set for yourself, because no matter what it is that you look at in life, there are going to be those ups and downs, and I love how Naveen Jain puts it. "If you think about living life, you have a heartbeat, and if you look at your heartbeat on an EKG monitor it goes up and down, up and down. That means that you're alive. That means that you're living." I love that so much because that means that you're growing, you're going to have the ups and downs, but you need to look at every situation as a learning experience and not let it hold you back. It's being resilient.

Let's look at it like one of those punching bags that children play with, where you can punch it, and there is a weight in the bottom. You would blow him up and when you hit it, it would go down, but they would pop right back up, and you would keep on trying to knock it down, and it pops right back up, or think of a Weeble Wobble. Weebles wobble, but they don't fall down, right? So, you are the punching bag, you are the Weeble and life brings you all sorts of things that try to knock you down, but you get back up!

I want you to think about some goals that you have set for yourself, and ask yourself, were you resilient in coming back and saying, "it didn't exactly turn out as I had planned however it didn't turn out so bad either." Then set another goal for yourself to get to it if it didn't happen yet. Sometimes we just need to take those steps, and there's nothing wrong with setting large goals, as long as you can see the small win in moving towards the large ones.

The best advice is to find yourself a theme song that when you're feeling down or when you're feeling discouraged or feeling as though you won't achieve what you want to accomplish, you listen to that song, and it gets you back on track. I call it my anthem, and it helps me to get myself back into that mindset that I need to be in. My anthem is the song "Get Back Up" by T.I. If you've never heard it, look it up. As well when I need encouragement through challenges, I listen to the song "God Is in This Story" by Katy Nichole and Big Daddy Weave. For me, these songs just get me back to a point where I believe in myself, where I come back, and I am resilient. I recover quickly.

You will know who those people are that are going to stand by you, help you and be a part of your life to support you, and those that are just there during the "win," that aren't really your friends. There will always be people that celebrate when you are down because your setback makes them feel good about themself. You have to ignore those people and surround yourself with the people that support you and celebrate you when you're up or down, no matter what.

If it's only you then that's ok, have faith, because there is God, and he will walk you through it. If you don't believe in God, then you have to find some other intrinsic internal motivation to stay confident and believe in yourself and know that you can do it.

The Story of Scott Lumley
When You Are Struck So Hard,
It Almost Kills You

"If you take the experiences of your past, and you live in the moment, that becomes your future." – Scott Lumley

Resilience would be the defining word for this man if I had to choose one for him. Scott Lumley grew up in great turmoil; however, he was a passionate young boy and very strong willed. He took care of his 2 younger brothers because they were very much neglected by his mother, who struggled herself throughout life while his father was in and out of jail. He often witnessed his mother as a victim of domestic violence going from one bad relationship to another. There were even moments whereas a young boy, he had to intervene because some brutally hurt her right in front of him.

Scott had no choice but to take care of his brothers from a very young age, and this is where much of his strength came from. He was the one that cooked, cleaned, got them ready for school, and prepared their food when they had any. They lived in hotel rooms or trailer parks, whatever they could afford. He would even go to yard sales to find clothes to wear, when necessary, as they often only had one or two pairs of pants.

At 11 years old, he ran away after a huge disappointment. He was working for neighbors and saving money for bicycles for him and his brothers, so they wouldn't have to ride the bus to school anymore. However, one day he got home, and the money was gone. His mother had used it for rent. Crying and sad, he went to fix his brothers' dinner, but there was nothing to eat. The refrigerator was empty, and there were just boxes of cigarettes on the counter. At this point, Scott had it, and he left. He stowed away in the luggage rack of a Greyhound bus and left to find his mother's ex-boyfriend.

When he arrived in Tulsa and found the man, his girlfriend at the time wanted nothing to do with him, and he was alone. He then met a preacher who initially helped him by giving him a place to live, food and some work to do. However, once the preacher called his mother, and she didn't care if Scott stayed or came home, the preacher realized no one would be looking for him, and this is when tragedy struck.

The preacher kept Scott chained in a barn for almost five years. When Scott finally managed to break free and escape from the preacher, he thought he beat him to death, and he never looked back. He made his way to working on a ranch and learned to ride bulls. He was then reunited with his father and had the opportunity to attend a private school as a teenager, but he barely knew how to read and write. Although he failed to get accepted, the head of the school was the only one who knew Scott's story and allowed him to study at the school and play baseball.

This was a great opportunity for Scott to attempt to have a "normal" life and get an education. However, most teenagers go to school, study, and possibly have a part-time job or do some extracurricular activities. Scott had to do all these things, and he was responsible for paying his tuition and his living expenses. He was the janitor at the school; he took care of the baseball field, went to class, studied, played baseball and on the weekends worked at a ranch and rode bulls. Not exactly a carefree, go-lucky teenage life.

Scott had an entrepreneur spirit at heart and started a landscape business during his senior year in high school among everything else he was doing. His work ethic, drive and motivation were astounding for the trauma he lived. He doesn't know where it came from, but he imagines it came from his desire to never take for granted the second chance that life had given him and never want to be dependent on anyone else.

The years to come were not always met with great opportunity, and he still lived with the trauma of his youth. He even tried to commit suicide later in life, but Divine Intervention came in a telephone call that saved his life in the moment he was going to take it. This moment made him realize he was given yet again another chance and was even more motivated than ever.

Over the years, Scott has owned different businesses. Some did well, and some did not, but he welcomed the failures as learning experiences. Today he is quite successful and helps other entrepreneurs build their businesses. He is also an advocate for human trafficking and suicide prevention, as these two issues are rampant throughout the world today, and he feels he can help by sharing his story with others to raise awareness and money to give to charities that focus on these problems, because the number of children whose parents are trafficking them is shocking. Just as shocking are the number of children who just disappear, like Scott, because no one cares if they disappear or not. What an alarming thought!

Scott's advice for young people is to quit putting pressure on yourself thinking that you have to know what your future holds. You don't have to know. Live in the moment, and everything will become clear as you move forward. He learned this from a spider when he was chained in the barn. He watched this spider build webs and wondered how it knew what it needed to do to survive. Scott attributes his learning of processes and strategies to the observation of this small creature. The lesson learned was to be present and aware of your surroundings. Pay attention to what happens in the moment and work the process. Don't worry about the future or the past, just focus on the present. "If you take the experiences of your past, and you live in the moment, that becomes your future."

16

What If I Succeed?

"Whether you think you can or think you can't, either way you're right."
— Henry Ford

How often do you say, "I can do that, no problem?" How about, "I can't do that, it's just too hard. I don't know how?" Whenever you say either of those statements, you are absolutely correct. If you say you can, you can. If you say you can't, you can't. It's that simple.

Often, we stop ourselves from doing something because we say, "What if it doesn't work? What if I apply for that job, to that university, and I don't get it? What if I try out for that team but I don't make the cut? What if I start writing that book but nobody buys it? What if I create this new business and it fails?" It's interesting how we are able to always bring to mind the doubt, the "what if it doesn't" instead of "what if it does or what if I do…?" You need to start saying, "What if I do get that promotion? What if I do get into that college or university? What if I do make that team? What if I do write a best-selling book? What if my idea is great?"

When saying what if it doesn't, make sure that you also think about, "What if I do succeed," and put that vision in your mind of actually accomplishing what you are thinking about. I like to think of a car, driving on the dark road at night, and you can see just the headlights and about ten feet in front of you. However, it's interesting that we never say, "what if the road isn't there," and we stop and turn around.

We don't do this because when we drive somewhere at night, although we can't see very far in front of us, we know that the road is there, and we know that we're going to get there, which is why we continue to drive. So, look at that as a goal that you have set for yourself. A lot of times people stop in the middle of what they're doing because they don't know necessarily how they're going to get there. However, if you look at the path to your goal like this car on the road at nighttime, where you can only see a little bit in front of you, but the rest is completely dark, you can say, "I know that the road is there. I know that the steps are there. I just need to trust that how is going to come." Just like that road continues to come mile after mile, the right things and the right doors are going to open for you as you continue on your journey to achieve your goals and dreams.

So, the important lesson that everyone should take away is, when you say, "what if it doesn't happen," and you know you're worried about being embarrassed, or you're worried about failure, or you're worried about what other people will think, say to yourself, "What if I do succeed," and think about what that would look like and what that would feel like.

Surround yourself with like-minded people. Often, the people that are closest to you will say, "Well, what if it doesn't work? What are you going to do? What are you going to have? How are you going to take care of yourself," and those things get in your head, and they can be scary. So, then you begin thinking, maybe I need to take the known road. Maybe I need to play it safe and take the short street that you can see from one end to the other, instead of the dark highway where you can't see the end of your destination from where you are standing, however you know it's there.

Think about reaching the end, reaching your goal and your destination. When you think about that and the impact it will have, you will want to continue saying, "what if I do succeed?" Think about it… at least for myself, when everything does work, I will be impacting millions of young people, they'll have a different future just because I didn't say, "what if I don't succeed?" I continue to tell myself it will happen because what I'm working on right now is going to impact a lot of people, and the only reason it won't work would be because I kept listening to my own self-doubt. I believe that it can work, that it will work. I will accomplish the goal I have made for myself. It's hard; it's a struggle. Sometimes you will want to throw in the towel; sometimes you will cry, but then I look for inspiration in the stories of others, and it is the fuel I need to keep going.

For those of you that are just starting out, and you keep on having setbacks, remember that setbacks are ultimately set ups. They're learning experiences, but if you allow a setback to merely be something that turns you around and stops you from continuing, instead of continuing to forge through it, you are always going to continue to ask yourself, "What if I didn't stop? What if I did continue? What if I was successful?"

We don't want to live a life that's full of regrets. Accept that sometimes things don't go right the first time, or maybe the second or third or tenth time, but if you believe in your dream, it will come. The one thing that is true about those that have had success in achieving their goals is that they did not listen to naysayers. They did not allow others to get in their head; they took the suggestions; they kept the ones that would help; and they left the ones that would hurt.

So, just remember the road to your goals or your dreams is not an easy one, but don't stop the car in the dead of night and turn around and go back. You are your vehicle. You may get lost along the way, you may have detours, it may not go exactly as you planned, however be open to the journey. God and the universe are your GPS. When we don't know the way in our car, we turn to our GPS, and it takes us in the right direction, and we know we will eventually arrive, even if it is a different road.

Your plan doesn't have to go exactly the way you picture it in your mind. Your plan might need to detour and have a different course because that's what is meant to be. Have faith in the process. Have faith in that maybe you don't know exactly how you will get there, but you know where you want to get to in the end and know that you can do it. You will most likely be "rerouted" along your journey, but the final destination will still be the same.

Now take that first step. Say, what if I do succeed, instead of what if I don't. Make that list, create that vision board, and take action. You can't fail until you quit. You can only learn, and at least you will always know that you did your best to get there and not live with regret.

The Story of Lee Duncan
The Road to Success Is Paved in Different Ways

"I want to make sure people are working towards their potential and not to their ability. People are able to do so much more than they believe."
— Lee Duncan

Lee Duncan was born and raised in Sheffield, England. When he was a young boy, he used to spend a lot of time every other weekend going to his grandparents' house because his mother and father were very strict with him and his brothers. His grandfather used to be a big sports fan, so he used to watch soccer and boxing with him, but every time the boxing came on, he used to get excited to get up and start moving around, and he just fell in love with it. It's from then that he started getting the vision of what he wanted to be.

Lee did not do well in school; his academic life was a total mess and as time went on so was his relationship with his father. The vision Lee had in his head of what he wanted to do was not what his father envisioned for his son. His father was in general a very negative person and his mother was a very positive person. His mother was his best friend growing up, and she always pushed him towards his vision by telling him he can do whatever he wants to do.

Lee used to battle with his father all the time because he wanted him to do what he wanted him to do. At the age of 16, he left school, and he left home to pursue his dream of becoming a boxer. Lee didn't know anything about living alone nor did he know how he was going to do it. All he knew was that he wanted to begin the quest and the journey to better his life and live out his vision of becoming a professional boxer.

At the time Lee was moving out, he came across his mentor who explained to him that certain things are hard to do, but he would have to do them if he wanted to better his life and become a success. Lee remembers waking up on the day he moved out and his father couldn't understand why he would want to leave when they had just moved to a more affluent neighborhood, but for Lee, he was a prisoner in his own mind at the time because nothing was happening for him, and it wasn't about being comfortable and having things, and once he left everything started to unfold.

His mentor helped him find a place, and when Lee moved out, he was around other athletes, living with athletes and world champions which was a major shift in his life. He attributes his success to being around these champions and other like-minded people because he then felt he could do it as well.

For Lee, motivation is not enough. Discipline is not enough. It has to be in your culture; it has to be a habit, a lifestyle. Whenever he tries to do something, he takes out the word try, because for him try means that he doubts himself, or there is the possibility that he won't be able to do it. Therefore, instead of trying, he was in progress, always working towards his goal.

After time passed, Lee knew he could do anything he set his mind to. The important thing that he realized at this time was that he knew he couldn't box forever, and that all sports have an age limit. Therefore, while continuing to press himself hard in boxing, he also challenged himself and went back to school to get into college. He found the discipline within himself because he knew he wouldn't always be able to depend on boxing. He eventually got a bachelor's degree and then a master's degree. He became the first British professional fighter to get a master's degree while fighting professionally. Often people ask how he was able to do it. He says he doesn't know, and at the time, he didn't know how he was going to do it, but he just let his body do the hard work in boxing, and he let his mind do the smart work.

Lee urges young people to always follow their vision because dreams and visions are often extinguished at a young age by the outside world, especially by family members. He was told multiple times not to get into boxing by those around him, but he wants young people to understand that everyone has a different perspective and a different opinion, so be careful who you ask for advice on what you want to be or do.

When Lee went professional, he knew he had created his vision because he believed in himself and because he worked for many years, surrounding himself with the right people and adopting the right mindset. He says, "Youth need to understand, there will always be barriers; there will always be challenges; there will always be struggles, but it is what you do that gets you past them. You can either allow them to defeat you or you can overcome them and push forward to reach your goals and dreams. Remember that sometimes you have to do things you may not want to do, like a certain job, in order to get to where you need to be. The important thing is that it's ok, and it happens to everyone, as long as you don't lose your vision and stay there."

Lee won his International Masters Title at the age of 22. Today he is still boxing and still training. As well, he owns his own business in the health and fitness space. He continues to surround himself by those who are doing what he wants to do or those who have achieved what he wants to achieve. If you follow your vision, you will be successful. His advice to those reading this, "I want to make sure people are working towards their potential and not to their ability. People are able to do so much more than they believe."

17

The Story of Bruce Pulver
Use Your Words Wisely

"Your words matter, so use them well." – Bruce Pulver

I left the story of Bruce Pulver to the end of this book because he is so wise and knowledgeable when it comes to words. What we say on social media, through messaging or conversation can hurt someone just as much as physical pain. With our words, we can lift someone to believe in themself, or we can break someone to feel as though they are nothing. We often do this to ourselves, by speaking to ourselves in a way that we would never speak to anyone else. Why is that?

It's time to reflect on what we are saying not only to those around us but also to ourselves. Bruce was blessed to be born in a home with parents who embraced every day as a gift, never dwelling on the negative, always focusing on the joy of living. They lived this way because they knew how precious life was since Bruce's mother almost died giving birth to him.

After 25 years of working in Corporate America, Bruce was faced with losing his job, and he didn't know what to do, but what he did remember from his parents was the power of gratitude in life, working through challenges, never giving up, and his father's love of words.

Bruce woke up one morning with the word STRONG in his mind, and he took the word and separated it by letters and made a word from each letter:

S tand
T all
R emain
O ptimistic
N ow
G o for it

He couldn't believe the meaning it had behind it. After that day, he woke up each morning with a new word for the next 420 days. It helped him encourage himself and inspire others to realize how important words are. What he learned and what he shares in his book, *"Above the Chatter, Our Words Matter,"* is that the power of a single word can dramatically change your life. He looks to take the words and lessons that we hear every day to change our mindset and build a power mindset on our JOurneY to success. Even from the word journey he creates the word JOY because he believes in our journey, we should have JOY and the u-r-n-e begins the phrase "you are naturally enough." It's amazing!

According to research, we have anywhere from 25,000 to 50,000 thoughts per day, and when looking at the thoughts of adults, 70 percent of them are negative. The majority of children growing up think they are unstoppable, feel as though they are superheroes, so where does the negativity come from between childhood and adulthood? Over time we are conditioned and programmed to play it safe, be protective and stop dreaming or thinking we can be that "superhero" anymore. So, let's stop this from happening to you and create a great mindset. To create what Bruce calls a *Power Mindset*, he breaks things down into 5 steps:

<u>Step 1: Activate Our Actions</u>

How often do you say something and actually do it? The key is doing what we say we are going to do. It's about following through and taking action. For example, you say you are going to read twelve books in a year. You will have to forgo something in order to be able to do this. It could be eliminating 30 minutes of TV each evening, waking up 30 minutes earlier or going to sleep 30 minutes later. Whatever it might be, to achieve success in the goal you set for yourself, you have to activate actions, develop new habits and do it.

Step 2: Committing to the Commitment

You start to make a commitment not by just claiming a resolution but finding a real solution to a problem, a challenge, or an opportunity. If you commit to something for 21 days, it then turns into a habit, and a habit is something you do and by doing that habit for 67 days, it then becomes a lifestyle change going from what we do to who we are. You must keep the promises you make to yourself as a way to build self-confidence.

C ount on me
O wn the actions
M ake it a priority
M ake movement on it every day.
I nvest, implement and inspect
T eaches personal responsibility in taking ownership

Step 3: Embrace the Incrementalism

An increment is the amount or degree that something changes. Making small changes in your life and building a powerful mindset is mental. You have to master your mind to make those small beneficial changes.

Step 4: Become a "Yes, I Can" person in a "No, I Can't" world

People need to say yes first and figure out how later. Often, we stop ourselves from doing what we want to do simply because we don't have all the answers when we first think of it. So, we allow the fact that we don't know exactly how to accomplish our goals tell us that we can't do it. By saying "Yes I Can," it just means that you expect success in challenging activities now. If you start with a YES mindset from the beginning, then the rest will fall into place as you keep moving towards it. Beware of the blockers that come in the form of negative words with 'not' as they will pop-up often. If you "can't" do something one way, find another way by "untying the nots" in your vocabulary.

Step 5: The Get/Give Ratio

Bruce's dad said to him that the only time GET should come before GIVE is in the dictionary. Meaning always look to give and serve others first before you ask for something. If you bring value to others, it always attracts the right kind of people. Always show you are willing to do more than others, and you will always be recognized as someone who goes that extra mile to give before you are trying to get something.

Now you can create this power mindset and take all of the lessons you have learned from this book to create your success. Get out of your comfort zone, listen to your internal dialogue and understand the importance of positive self-talk. Take control of what you say and do. Don't worry about those around you and what others are doing. Follow your own inner voice and strength. Finally, you can start with a single word. Choose a word that you want to describe you. Take that word and write it vertically and use just the letters of the word to create another word or phrase that relates to how you would define that word for you. For example:

S   tate your goal, dream, or obsession
U   nleash your desire; how bad do you want it?
C   onfidence you can achieve it,
C   all to action; what will you do to achieve your goal
E   ncompass yourself with like-minded people
S   tay the course, persevere, never give up
S   Ucceed

Remember you can create a Power Mindset towards success purely by activating your words.

Conclusion

"The two most important days of your life are the day you were born, and the day you find out why." – Mark Twain

Always remember to be the best person you can be. Take the lessons you learned here and apply them to your life. Hopefully you have been able to see that no matter who you are or where you come from, you too can live the life you want to live, nothing can hold you back but yourself. You are worth so much more than you can even imagine. Remember to be curious, look for answers, don't take everything you see on social media or on other platforms at face value. Remember like an iceberg, we can't see everything that other people have been through to get to where they are today. There is way more beneath the surface that we can't see. Be true to yourself, be who you want to be, not a copy of someone else, and don't worry about what others may think.

Continue to grow and learn more stories of people you admire. Find out how they did it. I welcome you to listen to the actual interviews of the amazing people in this book and more on my podcast, *"The Secret to Success… Isn't So Secret!"* I assure you that all of the characteristics to achieve your goals and dreams are the same as theirs.

Life is a journey with multiple successes along the way. Consume content from the media that makes you feel good about yourself, that makes you believe in yourself. Just as the expression goes, "You are what you eat," you are also what you read and what you watch. Be happy with who you are, where you are, and understand that success looks different for everyone. I can't wait to see what you accomplish, and I truly hope you share your story with me someday!

ACKNOWELDGEMENTS

A special thank you to the amazing people I have met while writing this book, for allowing me to share their story in hopes it will help someone else along the way. Learn more about the authors:

Learn more about Greg Walker:
https://www.greginspires.com/

Learn more about Ungenita Prevost:
https://www.femmeglobal500.com/

Learn more about Jen Welter:
https://www.jenwelter.com/

Learn more about Barbara Majeski:
https://www.barbaramajeski.com/

Learn more about Herb Lang:
http://www.herblang.com/

Learn more about Mike Poglese:
https://www.instagram.com/mikepoglese/

Learn more about Altagracia Pierre-Outerbridge:
https://www.outerbridgelaw.com/

Learn more about Naveen Jain:
http://www.naveenjain.com/

Learn more about Dr. Ana Olivero:
https://olapediatrics.com/

Learn more about Ria Story:
https://riastory.com/

Learn more about Paul Kazanofski:
https://www.instagram.com/pauliekazanofski/

Learn more about Maria Trusa:
https://mariatrusa.org/ - https://yodigonomas.com/en/

Learn more about Jonte Hall at:
https://jontenotsosmallhall.com/

Learn more about Roberto Mendoza:
https://thechefheavenskitchenusa.com/

Learn more about Ram Castillo:
https://ramcastillo.com/

Learn more about Scott Lumley:
https://scottlumley.com/

Learn more about Lee Duncan:
https://www.instagram.com/lee_duncan305/

Learn more about Bruce Pulver:
http://abovethechatterourwordsmatter.com/

Learn more about Glenn Marsden and Imperfectly Perfect:
https://www.imperfectlyperfectcampaign.org/

ABOUT THE AUTHOR

Kristi Maggio is an entrepreneur in education, teen mentor, public speaker and author. She is dedicated to creating access to education and employment opportunities worldwide. For over 20 years, she watched many children fail and feel inadequate merely because they didn't fit into the traditional way of learning. As a result, she chose to take action and founded a school that gives students the tools to create success in their life no matter who they are or where they come from.

After starting Maggio Multicultural Academy in the Dominican Republic in 2016, Kristi's mission became clear, to impact the lives of 1 billion youth in the next 10 years by providing an educational program based on entrepreneurship, applied learning, mentoring, as well as graduating with a specialization. This way upon graduation, youth have the option to begin their career, start their own business, or go on to higher education. It has become Kristi's obsession, to make a new ecosystem that provides youth with the skills they need before graduating high school, as well as diminish generational poverty.

Kristi has had great success in building relationships. The content of the high school entrepreneur program comes from her interviews and relationships with some of today's top entrepreneurs and thought leaders. Kristi has been described by Naveen Jain as "a great example of someone who is humble, and someone who is so dedicated to helping young people be at their best. I have learned just as much, if not more from her, and how she operates, than I have given back to her."

Learn more about Kristi, her work, and youth programs: https://kristimaggio.com/